What People Are Saying About *Opening the Door to Major Gifts...*

John Greenhoe's donor-focused approach to major-gift qualification will help you raise more money. He shows you how thoughtful attention at the beginning of the major-gifts cycle will lead to big payoffs. A must read!
Harvey McKinnon
President, Harvey McKinnon Associates

I love John's approach. He has a knack for simplifying and explaining this most difficult—and frequently scary—process for so many fundraisers.
Gail Perry
Author, *Fired-Up Fundraising: Turn Board Passion into Action*

John's rigorous analysis of the qualification call is exactly th~ ~rt of meaty research that our development profession must stri~~ ~ on a consistent basis. I love that his materials c~~ ~~ ~ed right away. A great resource for both fle~~ ~rs.
Guy Mallabone
Consultant, Global Philanthro~

Cold calling can be the most challeng ~~ ~~ ~using money, but it is the only way we can increase the num~~ ~~ of new friends needed in our organizations. John's practical advice and simple scripts will put anyone at ease to make the calls—and achieve great results.
Laura Fredricks
Author, *THE ASK: How to ASK for Support for Your Nonprofit Cause, Creative Project, or Business Venture*

John Greenhoe's valuable lessons in major donor qualification are on point not only for North Americans but also for those of us in Europe and throughout the worldwide fundraising community. I heartily endorse his methods and am deeply appreciative to John for his willingness to advance our global resource development efforts.
Valerio Melandri
Director and Professor, Master in Fundraising,
University of Bologna (Italy)

I appreciate John Greenhoe's candor about the discipline that is needed for successful major gift qualification. At the same time, his book shows that the task can be very rewarding and offers information sure to increase every fundraiser's success.
Erin Minne
Vice President, Advancement, Illinois State University

John's passion for major gift qualification jumps off the page. His book provides rich context to this important work through his sharing of tools and through his experiences, good processes, wit, and some old-fashioned inspiration.

Deb Minton
President, Philanthropia Partners

The process of qualifying and beginning the conversation with prospective donors is essential for the field of philanthropy. Congratulations to John Greenhoe for his hard work in moving the fundraising profession forward.

Bruce Flessner
Principal, Benz Whaley Flessner

John provides a great resource that would be a welcome addition to any fundraiser's tool kit. Kudos for this effort to expand our profession.

Paul McFadden
President, Youngstown State University Foundation

John Greenhoe is a go-to guy when it comes to discovery calls. He has fine-tuned the methodology for this important task in the major gift process.

Peter de Keratry
Director of Resource Development, Archdiocese of Brisbane (Australia)

John's book is an inspiration for those who are committed to raising major gifts. Based on his experience, he's laid out an easy-to-follow guide to effectively create relationships with those individuals who can take your organization to the next level. This is a must-have for anyone new to fundraising or major gifts.

Liz Sheahan
Director, Transformational Gifts, Society of St. Andrew

John Greenhoe's strategic approach to discovery calls is brilliant in its simplicity. He clearly illustrates, in no-nonsense terms, how to be successful in kick starting donor relationships. This is a great addition to any serious fundraiser's bookshelf.

Paul Knudstrup
Author, *The 8 Essential Skills for Supervisors & Managers*

Opening the Door to Major Gifts

Mastering the Discovery Call

John Greenhoe, CFRE

Opening the Door to Major Gifts: Mastering the Discovery Call

One of the In the Trenches™ series

Published by
CharityChannel Press, an imprint of CharityChannel LLC
30021 Tomas, Suite 300
Rancho Santa Margarita, CA 92688-2128 USA

charitychannel.com

ISBN: 978-1-938077-10-4

Library of Congress Control Number: 2013935061

13 12 11 10 9 8 7 6 5 4 3 2 1

Printed in the United States of America

This and most CharityChannel Press books are available at special quantity discounts for bulk purchases for sales promotions, premiums, fundraising, or educational use. For information, contact CharityChannel Press, 30021 Tomas, Suite 300, Rancho Santa Margarita, CA 92688-2128 USA. +1 949-589-5938

About the Author

John Greenhoe, CFRE, is a senior advancement professional at Western Michigan University (Kalamazoo, Michigan) who has trained thousands in the art of major donor identification and qualification. Greenhoe has also raised millions of dollars for both large and small nonprofit organizations and taught fundraising master's level courses at two universities. A popular speaker, he has delivered national and international philanthropy conference presentations in North America, Europe, and New Zealand. Greenhoe began his fundraising career as director of development for the Greater Kalamazoo Area Red Cross, where he initiated comprehensive major gift and planned giving programs. He has a master's degree in philanthropy and development from Saint Mary's (Minnesota) University, which features a strong ethical grounding in its fundraising coursework. Greenhoe is a contributor to noted fundraising publications, including *newz viewz* (New Zealand), *VITA* (Italy), AFP's *Advancing Philanthropy,* and Stevenson Inc.'s *Major Gifts Report.* He resides in Kalamazoo with his wife, Gretchen, and daughter, Anya.

Author's Acknowledgments

I would like to thank and acknowledge all of my family and friends who made this book possible.

To Gretchen, my partner and wife, you are my love, my rock, an amazing confidant, and a great editor.

To Anya, my daughter, thank you for reminding me what is most important. Namely, to fully experience the joy of life and everything that it has to offer.

To my many fundraising colleagues, thank you for joining me "in the trenches." The list starts, but certainly does not end, with past and current mentors at Western Michigan University.

To Bud Bender, former WMU vice president of development who retired in 2010 after a great career, you taught me much and challenged me to take on the task of conducting ID calls with discipline and vigor. Thank you for your service and inspiration.

To current WMU vice president, Jim Thomas, thank you for your courage and unflagging enthusiasm. Your support is deeply appreciated.

To my international colleagues (including the folks at the Fundraising Institute of New Zealand and the Festival del Fundraising, Italy), thank you for sharing your experiences. You have greatly expanded my horizons and encouraged me to explore new ways of thinking about our profession.

Finally, to my North American colleagues in the fundraising trenches—most notably my classmates from Saint Mary's (Minnesota) University—thank you for your counsel, advice, and wisdom. Together, we truly are making our world a better place.

Publisher's Acknowledgments

This book was produced by a team dedicated to excellence; please send your feedback to editors@charitychannel.com.

We first wish to acknowledge the tens of thousands of peers who call charitychannel.com their online professional home. Your enthusiastic support for the **In the Trenches**™ series is the wind in our sails.

Members of the team who produced this book include:

Editors

Acquisitions Editor: Linda Lysakowski

Comprehensive Editor: Jill McLain

Copy Editor: Lynn Pitet

Production

In the Trenches Series Design: Deborah Perdue

Layout Editor: Jill McLain

Proofreaders: Linda Lysakowski, Jill McLain, Stephen Nill, and Lynn Pitet

Administrative

CharityChannel LLC: Stephen C. Nill, CEO

Marketing and Public Relations: John Millen

Contents

Summary of Chapters

Chapter One: The Challenge Facing Many Nonprofits. The discovery call is a fundraising tool that is often overlooked, but you can use it to begin to build a relationship with your prospect.

Chapter Two: Getting to Know Your Donors. Learning as much as you can about your prospects prior to the first personal contact will increase your chances for success.

Chapter Three: Overcoming the Obstacles. There are many ways to "warm" the first call, including tapping your volunteers and donors to help make connections.

Chapter Four: Getting Ready. Having the right frame of mind is critical to the discovery call process. You can prepare your prospects for direct contact through letters, postcards, emails, and faxes.

Chapter Five: Let Your Fingers Do the Walking. Being regimented in making phone calls to prospects is vital. Know what you are going to say before you pick up the phone.

Chapter Six: The Gatekeeper and Getting Through. Many of your best prospects will have a gatekeeper who filters phone calls and other methods of contact. Secure the meeting with your prospect by emphasizing convenience.

Chapter Seven: Getting Ready for the Meeting. The impression you make is of utmost importance. Show respect for your prospect's time and let your prospect choose the meeting location.

Chapter Eight: The Visit. Conduct a discovery visit that is casual but purposeful. Consider using a list of standard questions for a productive visit.

Chapter Nine: After the Visit. Complete a discovery call report that will help you form a strategy and plan next steps. Be sure to thank your prospect by mailing a thoughtful and sincere note.

Chapter Ten: Following Up. Prepare a cultivation plan following the discovery call, but don't overthink it. Carefully consider the prospect "team" as well as who to bring to the next meeting.

Chapter Eleven: Trends and Topics. There are various factors to keep in mind when making qualification calls, including age of the prospect and type of nonprofit. Future trends in electronic giving, special events, and competition for major donors should be taken into account.

Chapter Twelve: Conclusion. Being both resilient and enthusiastic is critical to building new donor relationships. Above all, remember to enjoy the journey.

Foreword

As president of the Association of Fundraising Professionals (AFP), I'm always looking for ways to introduce new and innovative learning opportunities to our constituents. For that reason, I'm honored to be a part of John Greenhoe's book centering on the qualification of prospective major donors.

With each passing year, we are seeing increasing specialization and growing expertise within the development profession. This is very good news, not only for those of us here in North America but also for the entire fundraising community globally. In this context, it is especially important that we reach across continents to share best practices in an international context. Indeed, AFP's mission statement notes that we are an association of professionals "throughout the world."

It is my sincere hope that the lessons contained in this publication can be shared as widely as possible as we seek to promote the international availability of fundraising "tool kits." A critical topic such as major donor qualification—the beginning of a cycle that can lead to monumentally impactful partnerships and investments—is one example in the body of our work that we need to effectively impart globally.

Thank you for reading this book and for all of your efforts to advance our fundraising profession.

Andrew Watt, FInstF
President and CEO
Association of Fundraising Professionals

Introduction

This book provides an answer to a problem. A problem I faced a number of years ago and that many others face today.

In 1998, after nearly two decades of working in the communications field, I took the plunge into fundraising and began work as director of development for the Greater Kalamazoo (Michigan) Area American Red Cross. Simultaneously, I began pursuit of a master's degree in philanthropy and development at Saint Mary's University in Winona, Minnesota.

Previously, I had supported development functions as public relations director at Kalamazoo College, writing a number of media releases announcing major gifts to the college. As an outsider, I had been intrigued by the fundraising profession and finally decided to make the jump.

While I enjoyed the opportunity to raise funds for the Red Cross, which has a great mission, I quickly learned that it was harder than it looked. Since I had learned at Saint Mary's that "people give to people," I initially set out a plan to meet one on one with as many of our current donors as possible.

I found that setting up meetings, especially meetings with individuals who were not personally connected to our Red Cross chapter, was a difficult task. It took a great deal more time than I had anticipated to arrange for the meetings, and a number of people I contacted either did not want to meet or did not have time to meet. The challenge was complicated by the fact that major gifts was just one of my fundraising responsibilities there—a commonality that many one-person development shops face.

In 2001, I was thrilled to return to my undergraduate alma mater, Western Michigan University, as director of development for the WMU College of Education. While I was fortunate in my new duties to be able to focus solely on major gifts, I faced the same resistance from prospects. It remained quite difficult to schedule meetings—especially introductory meetings. During my first year, it was tough going, to the point that I was getting rather discouraged. While it had long been my goal to return to WMU, this was not proving to be my dream job.

All along, I kept thinking, *there has to be a better way*.

This book is "the better way" I discovered on my professional fundraising journey.

Some of the information in this book comes from the school of hard knocks. I kept trying different ideas until I found one that worked. I learned other methods from professional colleagues. For example, the discovery call questionnaire in Chapter Eight originated from a document shared with me by my former boss, Bud Bender, who retired as WMU vice president for development in 2010 after a long and successful career in fundraising.

As I'm sure you know, if you are not feeding new prospective major gift donors into your pipeline on a regular and systematic basis, sooner or later your efforts are going to stall. So, whether you are new to fundraising or have been active in the profession for years, this is a resource that can help you build new relationships and add good prospects to your portfolio.

The book provides specific strategies that will increase your odds for success when you are ready to meet your donors. You will learn—as I did—to "warm" your prospects so they are receptive to your outreach, to make allies of the gatekeepers who control access to the decision makers, and to conduct a qualification call that is both casual and purposeful. All of these methods are designed to initiate a comfortable and meaningful relationship that will one day result in a significant philanthropic investment.

How important is the task of mastering the discovery call? Take a look at the average portfolio of a major gift officer. A number of industry benchmarks indicate that if there are 150 individuals in a fundraiser's portfolio, as many as half of them (seventy-five) might be prospects/suspects who haven't yet been properly qualified. Therefore, it is critical for today's development professional to become proficient in prospect qualification.

My aim with this book is to present information in a straightforward and logistically sequential fashion. We'll start with the reasons why qualification calls are important and then delve into researching your prospects. Following that are practical tips for negotiating voice mail and gatekeepers en route to successfully making the appointment.

Next we'll focus on the actual format of the discovery call, including suggested scripts that you may wish to employ during your face-to-face visit. Down the homestretch, we'll look closely at strategies for conducting follow-up calls and then conclude with a look at future trends.

The qualification of donors is, generally speaking, not an easy task. Hard work and discipline are essential. At the same time, bringing new donors to your organization can be a lot of fun. You'll meet some amazing people, many of whom will share your passion for your nonprofit.

Bottom line, if you follow the strategies detailed in this book, I believe you will be successful. If I did it, you can too.

Thanks for reading, and enjoy the journey.

Chapter One

The Challenge Facing Many Nonprofits

IN THIS CHAPTER

···➔ A missing fundraising resource

···➔ The challenge of the discovery call

···➔ The author's "qualifying" experiences

···➔ Importance of the introductory call

I'm really fortunate to have received a lot of help in my fundraising career. I've had a number of great mentors and outstanding resources, including the master of arts in philanthropy and development program at Saint Mary's (Minnesota) University, that have boosted my efforts. Still, anyone in this business knows it's ultimately plain old hard work, some trial and error, and a good deal of dogged determination that lead to success. All along the way, I repeatedly heard and learned about the importance of building relationships with individuals who might one day consider making a transformational gift—a "major" gift.

In my many years of attending professional fundraising conferences, I have participated in numerous sessions focusing on major gifts. I have also participated in sessions on moves management, cultivating donors prior to solicitation, and stewarding them once the gift has been made. All of these topics are incredibly important. I have also read a number of top-notch books focusing on the solicitation process, or "the ask." Again, these are great "go-to" reservoirs of knowledge.

Identification, Qualification, and the Discovery Call

All three of the above terms will be used interchangeably in this publication, as is generally the case within the fundraising profession. All are essentially concerned with determining if an individual has the capacity to make a major gift as well as the inclination to do so.

While the word *qualification* may be the most technically precise of the three (we are qualifying a person's potential to make a significant philanthropic investment), *identification* is also a valid descriptor in that we are attempting to identify a prospect's interests.

Personally, I rather like the phrase *discovery call* because it seems very user friendly. After all, who doesn't like meeting new people and discovering new things? Sounds like a lot of fun, doesn't it?

finition

Despite these comprehensive learning avenues, I feel there is an aspect to the major gifts process that has been widely ignored. I have talked with dozens of fundraising colleagues about the issue, and they are all in agreement. This book attempts to fill that void.

Put simply, there is limited information available on the very root beginnings of the major gift process. Database screening and volunteer review sessions are great for determining who our prospective major gift donors are, but these exercises are worthless if we never actually reach out to these individuals and introduce ourselves. And therein lies the difficulty for even the most experienced of development professionals. *Initiating the process through an identification or qualification call can be a challenging task.*

Many in the profession will tell you that the door-opening call is *every bit* as difficult as asking for the gift. In fact, the Association of Fundraising Professionals (AFP) conducted a 2011 survey in which respondents indicated "making a call to a prospective donor" (ID/ qualification) was even more stressful than "making an ask" (face-to-face solicitation)!

Recently, I presented a webinar on the topic of this book. Afterward, I received a very nice email from a young woman who indicated she was new to the fundraising profession. In the message, she expressed thanks for helping her feel more comfortable about a topic that seemed "overwhelming and scary" to her. If this book helps even one more person become more at ease when considering ID/qualification calls, I will consider it a success.

The Challenge

Let me illustrate what I believe to be a huge challenge for many nonprofit organizations by relating what I faced in my first fundraising job. When I worked for the American Red Cross, one of my primary duties was to initiate a major gifts program. Although the Red Cross chapter I worked for had recently completed a successful campaign to build a new headquarters facility, it was obvious to me that while major gifts were raised for the campaign, there still wasn't a long-term plan for major gifts on a continual basis.

Further, it was clear that many of the donors (mostly corporations and foundations) who made larger gifts to the campaign were probably not ongoing candidates for major gifts, at least not until we had another campaign for bricks and mortar. What I did learn was that many of our best prospects for long-term cultivation of major gifts were not nearly as close to our organization as we might have liked. Some had been to our headquarters, and many had volunteered once or twice, but their primary contact was the annual fund direct-mail letters they received. They supported us, some very generously, but they really did not *know* us.

> ### AFP Quick Poll, March–April 2011: What causes most apprehension?
>
> Twenty-six percent—Involving Board in Fundraising
>
> *Twenty-five percent—Calling on a Prospective Donor*
>
> Eighteen percent—Making the Ask
>
> Twelve percent—Writing a Grant Application
>
> Eight percent—Other
>
> Six percent—Writing Fundraising Copy
>
> Five percent—Using New Technology
>
> **observation**

My "Qualifying" Experiences

In 2001, I came to Western Michigan University (WMU) as a constituent major gifts officer, serving as director of development for the WMU College of Education. While our overall development program was more evolved than what I experienced at the Red Cross, I was nevertheless struck by the same phenomenon. It was true that many of our alumni liked us and generously supported us, but at the same time, they remained relative strangers to us. Many of them had not been on campus for twenty-five, thirty, even forty years. I was also disappointed to learn that our ongoing communications with these alumni through the mail and other methods was, at best, sporadic.

Today, there are many charitable organizations throughout the world that face similar situations. They have a solid annual giving program and direct-mail donor base that provide a relatively reliable source of income. For many, unfortunately, this source is becoming stagnant and is even declining. It is becoming harder than ever to acquire new donors through the traditional method of direct mail. New methods of electronic solicitation have shown promise for bringing new donor prospects to the organization, but the potential for substantial investments from these prospects will likely not be known until a personal relationship is established.

Regardless of how donor prospects come to an organization—whether through a special event, a direct-mail donation, or an online gift—they should be reviewed or screened to determine whether or not they might be financially capable of making a major gift. The review can be accomplished through a committee of volunteers with knowledge about the donor population, a wealth screening provided by a vendor, or a combination of the two. Unfortunately, while volunteers can be a knowledgeable resource, quite often they are reluctant to help you make personal contact with prospects. Further, while wealth screening can give you some indication of a prospect's ability to give, it tells you nothing about one's inclination to do so.

The Importance of the Discovery Call

If you believe a prospect may have the ability to make a significant gift, that individual should be qualified through a personal visit, the subject upon which this book centers. In addition to verifying capacity, the purposes of the qualification call are to determine (1) the strength of the prospect's interest in, or affiliation with, the nonprofit organization and (2) the prospect's inclination to consider a major gift, given appropriate cultivation.

Qualification Calls

Qualification calls should determine:

◆ Capacity

◆ Interest and/or affiliation

◆ Inclination

principle

In the end, these factors can be effectively assessed only through a face-to-face visit.

While more and more nonprofits have developed successful major gifts programs, some still have not made the leap. The challenge is to continue to develop our annual giving programs and look for opportunities for major gifts as individuals "bubble up" in our giving programs. For this to happen, we need to make the commitment to pursue major gifts through board involvement and appropriate staff resources. In times when budgets are very tight, that can be a bitter pill to swallow.

Where's the Payoff?

Do qualification calls really work? Why should you spend so much time initiating new relationships that might or might not pay off?

While there are no absolute guarantees, I'm here to tell you that, conducted strategically, a vigilant focus on qualifying new prospective donors is almost always worth your while.

My personal experience bears this out. In December 2003, I experienced a highlight of my fundraising career when I documented a total of eight major gifts in support of WMU. At the time, a gift or pledge of $10,000 or more was considered a major gift for the university.

There were two main reasons for this occurrence—one for which I can take credit and one that was largely circumstantial.

For more than two years prior to my big month, I spent a lot of time meeting prospective donors who had not yet been qualified. During this period, I traveled frequently to the far reaches of the country to initiate new relationships. There was scarcely a rental car company or major hotel chain with which I was not familiar. I estimate that as much as half of my work time was devoted exclusively to qualification calls.

Lest I appear overly boastful, I should also note that December 2003 happened to be the final month of a five-year comprehensive fundraising campaign to celebrate the university's centennial. Two of the eight gifts were secured before year-end, specifically because the donors wanted their gifts to be counted in the campaign totals. Of those two, one of the commitments was actually secured during a qualification visit—a rarity in major gifts work.

Despite the extra incentive of the campaign, I strongly believe all that time in airplanes, coffee shops, and living rooms paid off! The experience deeply influenced my views of what it takes to succeed in the fundraising community. It also initiated the process that eventually led to the publication of this book.

To Recap

◆ The topic of donor qualification is often ignored.

◆ Donor qualification must be a priority.

◆ Fundraisers often find discovery calls difficult.

Chapter Two

Getting to Know Your Donors

IN THIS CHAPTER

- ⋯➜ Donor-centric research

- ⋯➜ Determining motivation

- ⋯➜ Deciding who to see

L et's talk about the issue of research and how it can help you prepare to make contact. You want to understand, as early as possible, the potential interests and values of the prospective donor. We've all heard about the importance of being donor centric in our approach. That should happen from the very beginning because we need to provide a value proposition. As clichéd as it may sound, we really do need to step outside of ourselves and look at things from the perspective of our donors. We know they are busy. Family and job pressures, busy social lives, and a myriad of other distractions make the task of arranging a meeting that much tougher. When you think about it, we really need to create a compelling reason for that person to agree to open the door to us.

Motivating the Prospect

During my days in the WMU College of Education, when calling retired teachers, I often indicated that I would like to tell them about the college's commitment to building stronger public schools. In my travels, I also had an opportunity to reach out to non-education alumni and met quite a few business graduates. Similarly, I tried to think about what might interest those prospects. For example, when calling an alumnus of our marketing program, I might remark that I would like to tell this prospect about the university's recent branding effort in order to gauge the prospect's reactions and input. I found this to be a very effective door opener, and it would often lead to conversations about a gift to support the programs I mentioned.

While the intent of this book is not to focus on prospect research, there are many ways to gain information about the prospect before the first visit. If you have access to a prospect-screening service that can help determine potential wealth, great. Having said that, ratings are only an indicator and are not always accurate. Yes, I have at times found it helpful to know the approximate value of a prospect's home and property, which is typically publicly available. If you don't have access to a wealth-screening service, though, don't worry about it. It's a nice tool, but it isn't critical.

Deciding Who to See

Here's an example of how wealth screening might be helpful but certainly not vital. Let's say you have time to see only one prospect but have two individuals with potential on your list.

The first prospect has a wealth-screening rating for potential major gift capacity of $50,000 and has made an annual gift of $500 to your organization in each of the past three years.

The second prospect has a capacity rating of $500,000 but has not given to your organization at all in the last five years. Before then, there were only two previous gifts, both of them $25, and both were more than five years ago.

So, which prospect are you going to try to meet with?

Always start with your current donors. Bill Gates may have a lot of money, but will he really give any of it to your organization?

The first prospect will definitely be my top priority because the prospect is a donor and, on top of that, a donor of some consistency (three consecutive years). The second prospect may have greater capacity, but I have no idea if the prospect has any real interest in my organization. Previous gifts were not large for a donor of this potential, and they occurred some time ago.

That's why I think wealth screening and gift ratings are helpful but not necessarily essential. In this case, did the wealth rating/screening really matter? At its simplest element, if someone is supporting your nonprofit on a regular basis, why not go to see that supporter—if for no other reason than to simply say thank you? Makes sense, doesn't it?

To Recap

◆ Why would the prospect want to meet?

◆ Find a connection to your prospect.

◆ See your "known donors" first.

Chapter Three

Overcoming the Obstacles

IN THIS CHAPTER

···→ The myth of the "cold" call

···→ Volunteer help

···→ Your donors as door openers

···→ Challenging and rewarding

···→ Organizational buy-in

L et's go back to the point raised in the first chapter—that many fundraisers find the ID/qualification call intimidating. Some fundraisers even term such visits "cold" calls. In reality, however, if you spend some time in thought and preparation, very few of your first donor visits—if any—will truly be "cold."

For me, there is no such thing as a true cold call. It's entirely possible to build rapport with a current or potential donor before a face-to-face meeting ever occurs. We will explore that concept throughout this book.

The Volunteer Role

There are many potential resources to help you "warm" the qualification call. If your organization has active and involved board members and leadership volunteers, they can sometimes provide valuable information about a potential prospect. Sometimes your volunteer will even go with you on a call to make an introduction. I will caution you, however, that in my personal experience, I have found that helpful volunteer assistance is the exception rather than the rule.

Your Donors as Door Openers

> If you can enlist volunteers to help you with door-opening calls, great. However, my experience indicates that the majority of ID/qualification visits should be staff initiated. I have found this to be true both in higher education and in my experiences with the Red Cross. In the majority of cases, the professional fundraiser has to do the heavy lifting.
>
> practical tip

It should be noted that not all volunteers are created equal. The stellar exception to the staff-driven rule is to recruit the involvement of top-level donors. One of my secret weapons at WMU has been to employ a select number of our current donors as door openers. If you can entice even a few of your major supporters to reach out to their friends and provide introductions, that will often provide a significant boost to your major gifts program.

For example, while working in the College of Education, I met two delightful sisters who eventually agreed to create an endowed teacher education scholarship in their family's name. The sisters were so thrilled with their donor experience that they encouraged and assisted with my qualification and cultivation of a good friend of theirs. The friend, clearly motivated by the example of the sisters, was similarly pleased to create an endowed fund of her own.

Challenging and Rewarding

While donor qualification can be a challenging task, it can also be very rewarding, both personally and professionally. I have met CEOs of Fortune 500 companies, top-level entrepreneurs, professional athletes, and leaders of high-profile nonprofits in my years of conducting hundreds upon hundreds of identification calls. Many of these meetings led to stronger relationships being forged between my organization and the individuals I visited. In a significant number of cases, the qualification calls eventually led to major gift investments.

In reality, all you really need to decide whether or not someone should be visited is some evidence of loyalty to your organization (i.e., frequent annual giver) and a hint that there may be some wealth. The hint could be as simple as knowing someone's job title. There are plenty of Internet resources that indicate what an individual's annual income might be, based on occupation.

Perhaps you may have access to colleagues who spend part or all of their work time researching potential donors for you to visit. If so, that's terrific, because prospect researchers are great resources. However, if you don't have anyone assigned to prospect research, that's fine too. I am very fortunate to currently work for a university that does employ prospect research personnel, but I did not have any such assistance in my previous work with the Red Cross.

Even in my current role, I find much of the information I need to prepare for an introductory call on my own.

Just about all of us use common, free web search services (for example, Google) when researching prospects, and some of us employ subscription services such as LexisNexis® for the same purpose. Social media can also be helpful. In particular, LinkedIn can be a great resource to gain employment information, keeping in mind that not everybody uses that service. I have also used Facebook and Twitter, with limited success, in attempts to learn about the personal interests of prospects. Again, you will find that not everyone leaves a digital footprint, but social media can provide a piece of the donor research puzzle.

Buying In

I believe that, other than the fear of the unknown, there is only one major barrier to making successful discovery/qualification calls part of your fundraising operation. That barrier is gaining buy-in from your organization's leadership.

In a new major gifts operation, you are going to need to make a lot of discovery calls. Given that a first call rarely results in a major gift (although that has happened to me occasionally, and it might for you as well), you are not likely to see much incoming revenue from initial efforts. So, patience is required.

When budgets are tighter than ever, how do you justify such an investment? Why should your nonprofit spend money on a fledgling major gifts effort instead of plowing the funds into another direct-mail solicitation letter or special event that will yield at least a modest amount of income? Can you provide proof that a major gifts effort is a good idea?

Yes. It's quite simple, actually. You can use your organization's current cost to raise a dollar (CTRAD) to justify a proposed investment in major gifts. Here's how. Look at your organization's income and expenses from the most current fiscal year completed. Take the total amount of funds raised for the year and divide it by the amount spent on fundraising activities. If your ratio is lower than six dollars raised to every one dollar spent, chances are very good that you are not devoting enough resources toward developing the relationships that will eventually result in major philanthropic investments.

In addition to gauging your overall costs, you should also measure each individual fundraising method. Let's say your charity holds a major golf outing each year. How much money do you raise from the outing, and how much does it cost? Be sure to include the costs of staff time in the overall equation. Would it make sense to forgo the golf outing and instead focus more on major gifts?

So, let's say you have the go-ahead to begin, in earnest, a dedicated major gifts program. Just how much time should you devote to identifying and qualifying your prospects?

In general, all major gift efforts should be fairly evenly balanced among the four traditional fundraising stages:

- ◆ Identification/ qualification/discovery
- ◆ Cultivation
- ◆ Solicitation
- ◆ Stewardship

Let's consider a nonprofit that annually raises about $100,000 in gifts, primarily through donor mailings and special events. The nonprofit's annual fundraising cost is about $25,000. Dividing $100,000 by $25,000, the organization's total CTRAD is twenty-five cents, or for every one dollar spent, you raised four dollars. Pretty good, but with a focus on major gifts, you can do even better.

Example

Using that standard, approximately 25 percent of your time would be directed toward discovery calls. Having said that, one-quarter of your time may not be enough for a new major gift initiative. In my first job at WMU (director of development for the College of Education), I had a lot of prospects who had never been qualified and only a handful of known significant donors. During my first year, I spent close to half of my time on ID visits. That might be a bit radical for some organizations, but I can definitely see the case for a good number of new major gifts programs setting aside at least *one-third* of the available time for identification and qualification.

In the next chapter, we'll dive right into specific methods and examples that will set the stage for successful discovery calls.

To Recap

◆ Cold calls don't have to be cold.

◆ Your donors are great door openers.

◆ Donor qualification can be rewarding.

◆ Use cost ratios to justify major gifts.

Chapter Four

Getting Ready

IN THIS CHAPTER

··· → Having the right mindset

··· → Defeating the unknown

··· → Using the post office

··· → The electronic connection

··· → Faxing

t's pretty easy to overthink how best to prepare for contact with your donors and prospects. At the same time, a little strategy is a good thing.

There is a certain mindset I try to get into when I prepare to connect with a prospect. I want to project confidence in myself and the organization I represent. While courtesy is important, I am proud of the accomplishments of my nonprofit, so I am not going to apologize for reaching out. I'm also not going to assume that my outreach is causing some type of imposition. While it is always a goal to be respectful of other people's time, my time is also important. My goal is to bring my prospect something of value. If I am successful, the prospect will appreciate the invitation I have extended.

My observation is that new fundraisers sometimes fall into an "apology first" trap when taking on ID calls. When that happens, many people will sense that you are uncomfortable with the task at hand. In response, your prospects might also become uneasy, and as a result, they will be less receptive to your outreach.

Free Your Mind, and the Rest Will Follow

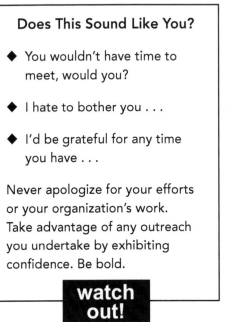

Does This Sound Like You?

◆ You wouldn't have time to meet, would you?

◆ I hate to bother you . . .

◆ I'd be grateful for any time you have . . .

Never apologize for your efforts or your organization's work. Take advantage of any outreach you undertake by exhibiting confidence. Be bold.

watch out!

So, what do you do if you are nervous and have a hard time extending yourself to strangers? Don't most of us have this problem?

While I am not advocating for you to be disingenuous, a modicum of acting can be helpful. Project the image you want to put forward, and practice it. This is something I frequently do when I get ready to pick up the phone. Some might call it "psyching" one's self up. We'll talk about this more in Chapter Five in our discussion of scripting your initial phone calls to your prospects.

Even before you make the call, try to put yourself in the situation of your prospect. If someone doesn't know you, how likely is that person to call you back?

No Surprises, Please

The unknown is the fundraiser's enemy when it comes to discovery/ qualification calls. You do not want your prospect to be surprised or somehow startled by your contact. You are, in fact, a stranger to your prospect, and your prospect has a busy life.

So, how do you overcome this challenge? You set the stage.

The Power of the Pen (and the Post Office)

In my experience, the best way to "warm up" your prospect for a phone call is to send something in writing beforehand. It could be a letter, a postcard, or even an email. For those of us who still use them, a fax can also be effective. The point is to give your prospect advance notice that you will be in contact.

I rather like good old postal mail—specifically, a letter—over electronic communication because I know that an email can easily get caught in a spam filter and never make it to its intended destination. I'm particularly opposed to sending a mobile phone text as an icebreaker. For me, that seems a bit too intimate coming from a stranger.

I tend to prefer letters because they stand out. Few people send letters anymore. I personally believe letters make a statement, mostly because you are taking the time to write the letter, put it in an envelope, and mail it. I believe that level of effort shows your prospect that you are a thoughtful person. As such, you are more likely to leave the impression that you are respectful and sincere. Doesn't that sound like a good starting point for creating a trustful and meaningful relationship?

The letter should be personally signed, and the envelope should bear an actual stamp (no postage meters). If your handwriting is crisp, I also recommend you personally address the envelope. If you do these things, most of the mail you send will be opened.

I've included an example here that I have used. I believe it is effective to have an authority figure make the introduction, but the letter could be straight from you, the fundraiser. At a bare minimum, it should state:

◆ Who you are

◆ What your purpose is

◆ Why the person being contacted (prospect) should respond/ participate

---

When you call for the first time, your prospect is likely to be thinking one or more of the following:

◆ *Do I know this person?*

◆ *Why is this person calling me?*

◆ *What is this person selling?*

◆ *What's in it for me?*

◆ *Do I have time to talk to this person?*

◆ *This better be quick.*

practical tip

As you look over the letter, you'll note that it clearly states my title (director of development) and the purpose of my work (increase private support). In the past, a couple of people have told me that my letter might somehow mislead the prospect into thinking my job is not to raise money. I disagree.

What the letter does indicate is that my purpose is to "determine perceptions" and "solicit input" regarding our programs. Absolutely true. Am I coming for the explicit purpose of asking for a gift? Of course not! If the prospect expresses interest in giving, great. But that's not my intention during a first visit.

When I make an initial call, I want to get to know the prospect and determine what is important to that person. Perhaps I will learn that my organization fits closely with the prospect's personal values, encouraging that individual to want to help us. Perhaps not. If I detect interest, I might start to think about potential projects for support, or ideas for involvement, but it is highly unlikely that I will propose anything on the spot.

The word "proposal" is a good one to describe what you as a fundraiser might take forward to a prospect at the appropriate time. I think a solicitation can be somewhat like a marriage proposal. Before you propose holy matrimony, you certainly want to take your time to get to know your intended partner, don't you? It's a big commitment, and there is much to be considered. In the same vein, isn't asking for a big gift during the first visit much like proposing on the first date? Both are inappropriate, and both seem destined for an unfavorable response.

Here's a letter I used early in my tenure in the College of Education at Western Michigan University. I thought it would be good to have a person of authority, the dean of the college, send an introductory letter prior to my phone calls (for the purpose of this sample, "authority" names are fictional).

Dear <name>:

Thank you for your interest in and support of Western Michigan University's College of Education. My purpose in contacting you is twofold. First, as you may be aware, President Bill Smith has determined that it is important for Western Michigan University to establish and maintain better contact with its alumni and friends. With that in mind, he has asked members of the university's staff to visit with alumni and friends associated with all ten of its academic divisions, including the university's largest and oldest college, the College of Education.

The second reason for this letter is that it also provides me an opportunity to introduce one of the newest members of the College of Education staff. Recently, John Greenhoe joined the COE team as director of development and will lead our efforts to increase private support. He is a 1983 graduate of WMU, and he recently earned a master of arts degree in philanthropy and development from Saint Mary's (Minnesota) University. John comes to our college with more than a dozen years of higher education and related nonprofit experience, and we are thrilled that he has come on board.

John will play an important role in our response to President Smith's call. I have asked John to contact a select number of alumni and friends who have significant connections to the College of Education over the next few months. John's purpose will be to determine perceptions and solicit input regarding Western Michigan University and, more specifically, this college.

John will be in touch with you to schedule a convenient time for a personal visit. While your comments will remain in the strictest confidence, they will be helpful as the college continues to formulate its plans for the future. I would be very grateful if you would make time for John in your schedule.

Once again, thank you for your interest and for your willingness to participate in John Greenhoe's work on behalf of the College of Education.

Sincerely,

Jim Johnson
Dean

In the sample letter, notice that the dean indicates he has asked the development officer to contact a "select" number of alumni and friends. By noting this, he is saying that the prospect is special, among a chosen few. He wants the prospect to know that not every constituent of the college will be personally visited.

While letters of introduction are great, they are just one approach. Another great use of our postal system in a more casual way is to send a postcard. For those of us who work in picturesque settings (i.e., universities with historic buildings familiar to alumni) postcards can be very effective. Other nonprofit sector ideas might be a postcard showing a "build" in progress for Habitat for Humanity or a child reading a book for a local library fundraiser.

I have tended toward the formal letter when planning to visit someone in an office setting, while the postcard seems to work better for constituents who might meet me in their homes. It all depends on your circumstances. In the College of Education, I met with a lot of retired teachers and school administrators, so I often used postcards.

Because it is more casual in nature, the postcard would come directly from me rather than a supervisor or other person of authority.

Postcard Example

Dear <name>:

Greetings from Western Michigan University! I work as director of development for the WMU College of Education and wanted to let you know that I will be traveling to your area (dates) and hope to connect with some of our alumni while I'm in town. There are some great things happening with our teacher education programs, and I would appreciate a chance to tell you about them if your schedule would allow. I'll be in touch soon to see if there would be an opportune time for a short meeting. Until then, thanks for your support and interest.

Best wishes,

John Greenhoe
(269) 555-6526

As you can see, the tone of the postcard is considerably more informal than the letter.

The question that follows is, of course, which is better? A letter or a postcard? Both have advantages and disadvantages. I urge you to think about your organization and your constituents to determine your best strategy. You may also want to test formats. Send letters to some of your prospects and postcards to others. See which group responds most favorably to your follow-up.

As far as the timing of your mailings, think about how many people you can realistically phone within a couple of weeks. Make sure you use a reliable calendar system to remind you of the needed follow-up. You don't want to send out a letter and determine afterward that you won't be able to call a prospect (or forget to call) in the next month.

Your strategy must also take into account your donor constituency with regard to geographic location. If you have a national constituency and you plan to travel significant distances to meet with your donors, you will want to target your mailings regionally in coordination with your planned travels.

Here's another idea. One of my former fundraising colleagues (Sherie Veramay, who succeeded me as the College of Education fundraiser) printed postcards with her head and shoulders photo on them. To see what it looks like, please refer to **Appendix A.** I thought the idea was a particularly good one for her. Our work in the college often brought us to the homes of retired teachers and school administrators as opposed to a business college fundraiser who might be visiting many corporate offices. If you are going to be sitting in a lot of living rooms, your prospects need to be comfortable with you. If you're trying to breed familiarity, what's better than sending a postcard bearing your smiling face?

Example

Here's an example. I used to travel from Michigan to California fairly frequently to meet with prospects/donors. In this case, I would send mail somewhere between a month and six weeks prior to my travels. Knowing that a postcard might take up to a week to arrive, I started calling about ten days after the mailing. My goal was to set up meetings in two weeks' to a month's time to coincide with my journey. My personal experience is that with many people, it's hard to get them to commit more than a month out, and less than two weeks is not enough advance time to secure an appointment.

You can also use a similar, more scaled-down approach if you have a statewide constituency. Just be realistic about how many people you can call or see in a given period of time, and you will be fine. In other words, don't send the letter if you think there is a chance you won't be able to follow up in a timely manner.

Selecting the Electronic Connection

I think "snail mail" is a great way to give your donor a heads up, but by no means is it the only method to get the job done. Electronic communication is certainly a viable option, even with the challenge of spam filters. I think email works well for busy executives because so many of them travel and may not open their paper mail for weeks at a time. One method I have used, with some success, is mailing the introductory letter a week or two ahead of time and then emailing the prospect a day before I call. The email says something like this:

> Hi,_____. I'm just following up on my recent letter. I wanted to let you know I'm going to try to reach you by phone in the next couple of days. If there is a particularly good time to connect, please let me know.
>
> John Greenhoe

The goal is to try to make it as convenient as possible for prospects. They may be much more willing to talk if you are not calling at a busy time, so give them the opportunity to tell you. If the prospect doesn't respond, go ahead and call.

I'm sometimes asked about social media. I think Facebook, Twitter, and other such avenues show promise for cultivation and stewardship, but I'm uncertain about using them for a first contact. A possible exception might be if someone is following you on Twitter. That typically means the prospect has something in common with you and might be receptive to your reaching out. A main drawback is that social media sites are publicly accessed, so know that if you write on a prospect's Facebook wall, the world can see it.

The professional networking site LinkedIn has potential, primarily because it's more akin to a business setting. I am aware of a small number of fundraisers who have used LinkedIn to set up qualification calls, but it has not yet been widely used.

If you attempt to connect with someone on LinkedIn (or a similar online professional networking resource), showing that you are affiliated with a cause that person believes in, such as alma mater, etc., might get you in the door. In general, however, my advice regarding the role of social media in setting up ID/qualification visits is to proceed *very, very* carefully.

Fax to the Max

Although I haven't done it extensively, I have occasionally used a fax as a means to warm up the first phone call. To me, a fax seems a bit unpolished compared with receiving a letter (perhaps because I have received too many unsolicited faxes for discount travel, printing services, and other things I do not need), but sometimes that is the best option.

You also need to take into account that, for some, the fax machine is outdated technology. It's pretty easy today to email a document as an attachment as opposed to faxing it. Still, it's an option. I can think of times when my research did not indicate a valid mailing or email address for a prospect, but I did have a fax number. If that is the case, certainly I am going to pursue the method most likely to reach its intended target!

To Recap

◆ Never apologize for your outreach.

◆ Letters and postcards can warm your contact.

◆ Sample documents you can adapt for your use.

◆ A letter from top organizational leadership can warm the call.

Chapter Five

Let Your Fingers Do the Walking

IN THIS CHAPTER

····➔ Pick up the phone!

····➔ The importance of voice mail

····➔ The message

True confession time. In my first days as a fundraiser, the thought of picking up a phone and calling someone I did not know was pretty intimidating. *Especially* calling someone I might ultimately want to ask for a gift! Since then, I have learned that I was not alone. Far from it.

As difficult as this task might first appear, I have also learned that it is an important skill to master. How did I come to this conclusion?

Over the course of my career, I have worked with dozens and dozens of colleagues at other nonprofits. While there are other traits that lead to success, I have determined one commonality I believe is essential. Fundraisers who are disciplined about calling new prospective donors typically fare well. Those who aren't usually don't last long in this field.

By and large, the most successful development officers I have worked with developed a regimented procedure for connecting with new prospects. In fundraising, the importance of the pipeline, and bringing new donors into it on a regular basis, cannot be overstated.

> ### The OARS Method:
>
> ◆ **O**ne Hour Each Day
>
> ◆ **A**t Least Seven Calls per Valid Prospect
>
> ◆ **R**ecycle Your Prospects
>
> ◆ **S**ee Them, or Cross Them Off

I have developed a very simple process for telephoning prospects that I call the *OARS* method. Here are the components.

"O"—One Hour Each Day

You must make time in your workday to make telephone calls to the prospects you would like to see. I recommend setting aside one hour in the eight-hour workday.

The time of day you schedule that hour is up to you and, to a certain extent, your prospects. I suggest you examine your work habits and determine when you have the most energy. If you are a morning person, by all means, make 8:00 or 9:00 a.m. the time for your calls. If you take a while to get up and rolling, aim for later in the morning or sometime in the afternoon.

Anyone who knows me can tell you I am not a morning person. Although I have made plenty of phone calls to my prospects first thing in the morning, it is not a time of peak efficiency for me. I do much better in the late morning or, even better, in the afternoon.

One of my favorite times to call is late in the afternoon. My preference is to call the prospect's place of employment first before trying a home or mobile phone number. The main reason for this is that I can usually find the business phone number most readily. If I can't get through at work, however, I will try to track down other phone numbers and follow up accordingly.

By later in the afternoon, I specifically mean the hour between 5:00 and 6:00 p.m. or just after the end of regular business hours. Why?

First, my experience has been that for many professionals, the period right after 5:00 p.m. can be a time when they are back at their desks, trying to catch up after a busy day. There are a lot of executives I have visited who are often away from their offices at meetings all day but then return after hours.

Second, after 5:00 p.m. is a time when I can usually bypass the gatekeeper or the administrative assistant who screens the calls made to my prospect. The same principle would apply to calling around 7:00 a.m., which is typically before the gatekeeper might be in the office. Many times, I have reached my prospect directly this way rather than having to negotiate with the gatekeeper. I'll write more about working with gatekeepers in Chapter Six.

An hour is plenty of time to make a lot of phone calls. You are going to get a lot of voice mail (more on that later as well) or gatekeepers, so generally you should be able to make at least one solid call every five minutes, or a total of twelve in an hour. Even if you don't reach any of your prospects directly, a dozen calls/messages is good progress toward strengthening your donor pipeline.

Some of the development officers I have worked with did not enjoy making these phone calls, nor did they have good strategies for making the calls. Because of this, they often struggled to have enough active major gift prospects who might someday make an investment. If you don't have new potential donors on the front end, you are in trouble. In that respect, major gifts work is like sales. It's a numbers game.

"A"—At Least Seven Calls per Valid Prospect

I recommend making at least seven telephone calls to a potential prospect before crossing someone off your list or marking that person for follow-up at a later time.

Why seven? The number might seem arbitrary, but practice has told me that seven is a good number. Further, in the marketing profession, it is generally thought that it takes at least seven phone calls to reach the average "C-level" executive (CEO, CFO, CIO, etc.).

Recently, a development colleague told me he finally reached a prospect with his seventh phone call. The prospect congratulated my colleague during the call, telling him, "If I don't know you, you are going to need to make at least seven (phone) calls for me to respond."

I can think of at least three development officers with whom I have worked in the past who complained to me that they couldn't get their prospects to return their calls. My response was always, "How many times have you called?" In all three cases, the answer was either two or three phone calls.

"That's not enough!" I retorted.

Let's face it, people lead busy lives. Chances are pretty good that the timing of your call will be inconvenient. So, keep calling. Eventually, you should be able to make a connection.

Some tips about those seven calls. First, it seems obvious, but don't call a prospect every day. That's harassment. A good rule of thumb is to try once a week. That's often enough to let the prospect know you are serious about coming to visit but far enough apart that you are still allowing your prospect a bit of comfort room. Second, vary the time of day you call the prospect. Call first thing in the morning, at noon, or in the early evening. If you move your call times around, you are going to increase your chances of getting through. Don't worry; I'm going to tell you what to say each time you have an opportunity to leave a message.

"R"—Recycle Your Prospects

Let's say you have called seven times and still have not reached your prospect. Time to cross that prospect off, right? Not so fast.

Have you considered the following?

- ◆ Your prospect is on an extended overseas trip.

- ◆ Your prospect just accepted a new job or promotion.

- ◆ Your prospect was recently fired/laid off.

- ◆ Your prospect has had a death in the immediate family.

- ◆ Your prospect is sick/in the hospital.

- ◆ Your prospect just got married.

- ◆ Your prospect is going through a divorce.

- ◆ Your prospect just had a baby or adopted.

There are any number of other possibilities, but you get the idea. If you were facing one of these challenges, is it possible that you might be hard to reach over, say, a two-month period?

I have personally experienced each of the above reasons for unreturned calls. In many instances, it wasn't that the person didn't want to talk to me. It was just a bad or very busy time in the prospect's life.

That's why if you reach the seven-call threshold and you haven't yet connected with your prospect, it may be wise to postpone contact until a future time. In other words, you should recycle your prospect. Perhaps wait three months, or six months, and try again.

As they say, "life happens." Keep your options open and come back later. You might just find that your prospect will be delighted to hear from you.

"S"—See Them, or Cross Them Off

The reality is, discovery/ qualification calls really are a numbers game. Let me give you an example. Let's say you are a major gift officer who is given a list of fifty people who may have major gift potential but need to be qualified. My experience indicates that no more than half of the people you

It seems as if every place in the world has some sort of precious and highly coveted commodity that is provided by Mother Nature. In Michigan, where I have lived all my life, it's the Petoskey stone. You typically find them in the northern Lower Peninsula along Traverse Bay. They are distinctive-looking little slices of nature, with hexagonal patterns, that you can find each spring after ice from the long winter has dragged up all sorts of matter from deep within Lake Michigan's waters.

When hunting for Petoskey stones, you have to be patient. Depending on the beach, you can look at a lot of rocks before finding a single, solitary Petoskey stone. It's cool when you do find one, however, and each one is unique.

I think that discovery/qualification calls, the first step in the major gifts process, can be a lot like looking for Petoskey stones. You have to sift through a lot of prospects to find that one unique individual who deeply believes in your cause and who is motivated to make a difference. Just remember to keep looking, because it *is* worth the effort.

are calling will eventually agree to see you. In other words, twenty-five of the fifty people will either be unreachable or refuse a visit. Perhaps you will do better than that. If so, kudos to you. Just remember that a .500 batting average for scheduling qualification visits is very good in this field, regardless of what might happen during the actual call.

Is the thought of crossing half of your new prospects off your list *before you even see them* discouraging to you? Don't sweat it. Most nonprofits have many more potential major gift donors than they have time to see. There will be an opportunity to add plenty more names to your list.

Although it may seem laborious, making lots of phone calls and crossing people off your list is part of the process. You will uncover some very good prospects along the way, but patience and persistence are essential. Especially with regard to ID/qualification, your list is going to be a continuous and moving target.

"Sorry, I Can't Come to the Phone Right Now"

As I mentioned earlier, when making phone calls to reach your prospects, you are going to reach a lot of voice mail. So, you will want to be well versed in leaving a brief but compelling message.

There are positives and negatives to reaching voice mail. On the plus side, you can use it to make a connection with a potential prospect on your time schedule. On the other hand, leaving a voice-mail message is no substitute for an actual phone conversation. Still, it is often the only way to make direct contact.

In today's impatient, distracted, and text-message-driven society, I think a good old-fashioned voice-mail message is still powerful. More and more, people are relying on alternative communication methods to get things done. Many people just don't have time to pick up the phone. For that reason, a voice-mail message can stand out.

As we discussed earlier, you will, of course, have mailed your prospect an introductory letter or postcard before your phone call. So you dial the phone, and you reach voice mail. What comes next?

Get the Message?

Well, I'll first tell you what *not* to do. What you should *not* do is hang up without leaving a message! I have had people in sales tell me you should never leave a message, that you should just keep calling until you get through. Their rationale is that you give up control when you leave a message. You are relying on the other person to respond. I understand the argument, but I still think it's a bad idea, especially for a fundraiser. I'll explain why.

We work for nonprofit organizations. Like it or not, because of this, we are held to a higher standard. We need to be as direct and up front as possible in presenting ourselves and our organizations. Personally, my first impression of someone who keeps calling me without leaving a message is one of distrust. When that happens, I typically think:

◆ Why does this person keep calling me?

◆ Why won't this person just leave a message?

◆ Do I really want to talk to someone who won't leave a message?

If I want to gain someone's trust, I think making a series of message-less phone calls is a bad move. Not only does it create mistrust, it's also annoying.

The reality is that many people today screen their phone calls. Leave a message!

I like to refer to a list I put together s a reminder when I am calling for phone appointments. These are my seven killer "BEs" for getting the return call!

BE Prepared

Have a plan for what you are going to say. You should have your message thought out well before you hear the "beep." An unscripted, unrehearsed message is likely to be unclear or rambling and will not result in a return call.

BE Clear

Use straightforward, simple language in your message. No jargon, technical wording, or acronyms. Say things in a way that your eighty-year-old mother or your eight-year-old nephew would understand. At this introductory stage, you cannot afford to confuse.

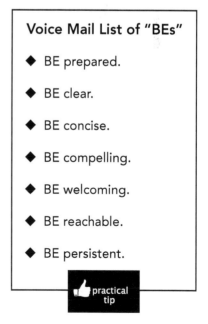

Voice Mail List of "BEs"

◆ BE prepared.

◆ BE clear.

◆ BE concise.

◆ BE compelling.

◆ BE welcoming.

◆ BE reachable.

◆ BE persistent.

practical
tip

BE Concise

State the main purpose of your call within the first fifteen seconds. Strive to keep your message to thirty seconds, with forty-five seconds as an absolute maximum. Speak slowly enough to be understood, and especially slow down when leaving your phone number. State your phone number twice— once early in the message and once again at the end.

> Don't you just love getting those telemarketing calls when you can tell the caller has delivered the same pitch, verbatim, hundreds of times? You don't? Then do not expect your prospect to react any differently. Know what you want to say, but don't read it. Just keep a 3 x 5 note card handy with the three or four things you need to get across in the message and refer to it if you get stuck. Make your points, but be conversational.

Leaving a message longer than thirty seconds is risky. Leaving a message longer than forty-five seconds is death. You really have to make it quick. You may be tempted to leave a longer message, thinking that a longer explanation of the reason for your call will increase the odds of being called back, but it won't. It will, however, increase the odds of your message being deleted and disregarded.

BE Compelling

Ask yourself a simple question. Why would the prospect want to call you back? If you have information on the prospect's expertise and areas of interest, find a way to connect that interest to your organization.

There are two ways to use your prospect's personal interests and expertise as motivators to engage with you. The first and best way is to present yourself as a person who has information that is valuable to the prospect. By calling you back, the prospect is going to gain something.

The second way is to ask for the prospect's counsel or advice. Let the prospect know your organization would benefit in some way by making a connection or by reconnecting. Most people are thrilled to impart knowledge in areas around which they have developed their professional careers.

The obvious caution here is that you need to be genuine. Be certain that your organization will make constructive use of the advice of your current and prospective supporters. If you solicit advice for the sole reason of getting to know your donors, your prospects will figure that out pretty quickly.

BE Welcoming

Even if you're having a bad day, you have to summon up all available positive energy when leaving the voice-mail message. Ways to accomplish this include:

Standing Up

One of my favorite strategies for injecting energy into my phone calls is to remain on my feet. Often that alone is enough to make me more alert. In turn, there is going to be more positive energy in my message.

Your Voice-Mail Message

Here's an example of what I might say (while I worked in the College of Education) when leaving a voice-mail message:

"Hi, this is John Greenhoe. I'm a development officer in the College of Education at Western Michigan University. My phone number is 269-555-6526. Mr./Mrs./Ms./Dr. _____, I believe you have a degree from Western in our college. I've been asked to contact some of our most outstanding alumni to update them on our latest education initiatives and also to ask for their advice. I'd greatly appreciate it if you would return my call at your earliest convenience. Again, my number is 269-555-6526."

Note that I would not read this word for word. This is only an example. Also note that I mention my phone number right away, in case the message is cut off for some reason. I say, "I believe you have a degree in our college," because in my situation, occasionally our records were incorrect. The person I called was likely a WMU grad, but sometimes the major was listed incorrectly.

Also note that this message is about thirty seconds in length and that I ask the recipient to do something—call me back. And I give my phone number again at the end, after I have given the reason for my call.

Example

> Look at the professions of your prospects and determine if they have expertise of value to your organization. Examples:
>
> ◆ Marketing—advice on communications/branding plan
>
> ◆ Finance—advice on investment strategy
>
> ◆ Human resources—advice on hiring practices
>
> ◆ Other professions—serve on advisory committee relating to expertise
>
> **Example**

Smiling

Here's an experiment that requires self-observation. Get an audio recorder and record yourself leaving two practice voice-mail messages. For the first message, make yourself smile, and force yourself to keep smiling throughout the message. For the second, deliver the message with a straight face. I'm guessing that when you play the messages back, you're going to prefer the first. It is simply human nature to sound more uplifting and energized when you're smiling. People respond to individuals who project a positive image. Sounds simple, and it's true.

Visualizing

Before you call, make the assumption that the person you are reaching out to will gladly respond. The more cynical readers of this book may roll their eyes at this suggestion, but it works. By imagining a positive outcome, you are going to project an energy that people will respond to.

The lesson behind these techniques is that your prospects will be left with the impression that interacting with you will be a pleasurable experience. It's really that simple. A welcoming attitude will attract positive responses. Just try it.

BE Reachable

If your prospect calls you back, you need to pick up the phone. Even if you have an administrative assistant to answer your calls, it's really better if your prospect can reach you directly. I suggest you leave your mobile phone number when you call and that you keep that phone handy at all times. If that's something you are not willing to do, I suggest that you are probably not cut out for this line of work.

Anything that will allow your prospects to reach you right away is to your advantage. It's fine to offer a best time for prospects to reach you, but as I just mentioned, you really should leave it open-ended and be ready to answer whenever they call.

If your prospect has any difficulty at all in reaching you, the chances of arranging a meeting are slim.

Many fundraisers work for small organizations where all phone calls are routed through one main reception line. If this is true in your organization, make sure your receptionist has clear instructions on what to say to prospects when they return your calls. Because some nonprofits use multiple individuals, including volunteers,

Make sure that anyone who might have an opportunity to speak with your major gift prospects knows what to say and how to reach you quickly.

important

to answer the main line, you should put the instructions in writing for the sake of consistency. You might even want to offer a training session for the folks who answer your main phone line.

BE Persistent

One can easily be discouraged in setting up first visits. Don't take it personally when prospects don't return your calls.

In making follow-up calls, you will want to reiterate your main message but be slightly more assertive. Your prospect's time is valuable, and so is yours, so get to the main point of your call as soon as possible.

One of the best compliments I have been paid as a fundraiser came from a wonderful gentleman I called upon who eventually became a major donor. In speaking with one of his friends, the donor said that I was "persistent but not pushy." I haven't always fared as well in building donor relationships, but apparently in the case of this person, I did it right. The subtlety of this point is, if you truly believe in your cause and your organization, you must be persistent. You have an important story to tell, and it is critical that people hear it. If you believe, you must persist.

If you want to cut through the clutter and stand out from your competition (and anyone else who is trying to get your prospect's attention *is* your competition), you must make voice mail work for you. Remember the first step is to get the attention of your prospect so you will get a call back. Again, you are selling yourself first. There will be plenty of time to discuss your organization during the face-to-face meeting!

To Recap

◆ Remember the OARS method.

◆ Be disciplined in your appointment-making approach.

◆ Use a donor-centric focus for getting return calls.

◆ Use a script when leaving voice-mail messages.

◆ Remember the seven killer "BEs" for making a connection.

Chapter Six

The Gatekeeper and Getting Through

IN THIS CHAPTER

····→ Befriending the gatekeeper

····→ What to say when you reach your prospect

····→ Make convenience a priority

One of the things I learned very quickly as a major gift officer was how to work with the administrative assistants of my prospective donors. People who are successful surround themselves with people who are sharp, are organized, and can save them time. These are the "gatekeepers," and they can make or break you.

In some ways, your relationship with the gatekeepers is just as important as your relationship with the prospects. You need to make them your allies. It is important that you take the time to learn about their interests, family, and anything else that is important to them.

If you have a comfortable relationship with the gatekeeper, this person can give you advice about the prospect. I like to ask gatekeepers about the best times and locations to meet with their supervisors. They can tell you if their bosses conduct meetings only in the office or whether lunch might be a better suggestion. In asking for guidance like this, I am showing respect for the knowledge the gatekeeper possesses while at the same time indicating that I want to act in the best interest of the prospect (requesting meeting times/locations that are preferred, convenient, etc.).

Motivating the Gatekeeper

One of the things I like to do in cases when I can't reach the prospect directly is see if I can enlist the gatekeeper as an advocate. I might call the gatekeeper and say something like:

"I know Sara is very busy, but is there any chance there might be a short window of time in her schedule to meet with me? She is truly one of our outstanding alumni, and I would really like the opportunity to reconnect her with her alma mater. Is that something you might be able to help me with?"

I'm trying to do two things here. First, I'm acknowledging the power of the gatekeeper. I'm telling the gatekeeper that I need help. Second, I'm trying to show the assistant that I am offering an opportunity that the boss might enjoy. My hope is that gatekeepers will realize it might be in their best interests to help me. I have found this approach to be an effective strategy.

 practical tip

To a degree, it's true that gatekeepers are intended to serve as buffers or filters for their bosses, but I believe if you can show them value, they will typically respond favorably.

Speaking with Your Prospect

Now, let's say that lightning strikes and you do reach your prospect with the first phone call. What do you say?

Remembering that you have already "warmed" the call with your introductory letter, postcard, etc., it's pretty simple. You are reiterating the messages you wrote in your introduction. The best approach is to simply ask for the meeting in a thoughtful but low-key way.

One of the best strategies for lowering any anxiety that prospects might have is to assure them they will enjoy and benefit from the meeting. You really do have to customize your approach from the "What's in it for me?" donor perspective. That's why it's good to hint at some of the exciting things going on at your organization, without going into detail. You want to intrigue your prospect enough to secure the meeting. Save the detail for the face to face.

As I noted earlier, you need to emphasize convenience. You must make it as easy as possible for the prospect to meet with you, but then take it a step farther. Show the prospect that the meeting is also convenient for *you*.

What do I mean? Here's an example of what I might say:

"I'm going to be in downtown Chicago visiting with some of our alumni on April 15 and 16. While I'm in the area, I was hoping I could schedule a short visit with you. Do you have any time during those two days when I could pop in?"

The message I'm delivering is basically that meeting with the prospect is pretty easy and convenient for me. It's not a big deal. Many of the prospects I have met would balk at the thought of my going way out of my way for a visit or coming to downtown Chicago "just to see me." If they did sense I was making a long trip just for our meeting, a subtle pressure could be created that would not be favorable to the discovery call. You want to diffuse such discomfort.

I believe if you remain as flexible as possible and see prospects on their own terms, the odds of scheduling a meeting increase significantly. I have met prospects in airport terminals, in subway train stations, on the beach, and on boats. These meetings all worked because they were convenient.

"Is This About a Gift?"

This is a question I would occasionally be asked when trying to schedule a discovery appointment. It's certainly not an unusual one, in that my introductory note indicates I am a director of development. Here's my answer:

"While a key goal of my work is to raise philanthropic support for Western Michigan University, I'm not coming to ask you for a gift. My purpose is simply to renew contact with you, to learn about your experiences as one of our outstanding alumni, and to bring you news from WMU."

If the prospect pushes back more, it's probably an indication that a meeting is not likely to happen or that a meeting will not be productive. I have, on a number of occasions, indicated to prospects that a gift discussion during a first meeting rarely happens and that when it does, it is always at the suggestion of the person I am meeting with. The subtle message is that asking for a gift would not be appropriate because we don't really know each other yet.

important

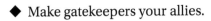

To Recap

◆ Make gatekeepers your allies.

◆ Serving the prospect's needs is key.

◆ Emphasize the convenience of the visit.

◆ Be flexible when choosing the meeting location.

Chapter Seven

Getting Ready for the Meeting

IN THIS CHAPTER

- ┅➔ It's about you more than your organization

- ┅➔ Setting the stage

- ┅➔ Printed materials

- ┅➔ The right location

o, your prospect has agreed to meet, and you have scheduled a time and location for the meeting. How do you prepare?

What I am going to explain next may initially cause some concern or confusion. As fundraisers, we are taught that our organizations should always be in the forefront. As fundraisers, we tend to work behind the scenes. It is not "about us."

When it comes to donor identification and qualification, however, we really need to flip the script. The discovery call is really very much about the fundraiser. We need to establish a personal relationship with the prospect and *then* let our organizations take center stage.

What you, the fundraiser, say and do—the impression you make—is of the utmost importance. Like it or not, for the purposes of the first meeting, you are the face of the organization. For example, as a university fundraiser, I eventually realized that my actions before and during the call often mattered as much as, or perhaps more than, the prospect's past relationship with the university.

Many of the individuals I visited had not been on our campus for thirty years. Even if their memories of being a student were positive, they were nevertheless fuzzy. In some respects, it was almost like starting a new relationship between the prospect and WMU. In such an endeavor, it was absolutely critical to prove myself a reliable and trustworthy person during the first meeting.

Prep Work

Let's delve into a bit of detail to illustrate my point. Following simple business etiquette can establish the foundation for success. Again, my initial goal is for the prospect to have a favorable impression of *me*. Shortly after arranging the meeting, I like to send an email (regular mail is fine as well) thanking the prospect for agreeing to meet, confirming the date and time, and so forth. Not only is the gesture thoughtful, but it also prompts the prospect to reconfirm the appointment. I hate to admit it, but occasionally (only very rarely, thank goodness), I make an appointment and then get sidetracked before I put it on my calendar.

Here's another tip for getting the appointment locked in. Assuming I have interacted with the prospect's administrative assistant in making the appointment, I will copy that person on my email message. There's a good chance the assistant is in charge of the schedule to begin with, so it makes sense to be sure the assistant is in the loop.

Here are a few ways to help show the prospect you are trustworthy as you (and the prospect) prepare for the visit:

Show Respect for the Prospect's Time

I have often used the strategy of suggesting that a meeting with me will take no more than thirty minutes. I will make that offer when I phone, especially with prospects I know are busy.

As an example, at one time I worked on a mock trial team initiative that had special appeal for the legal profession, so I met with a lot of lawyers. Because attorneys typically bill by the hour, I knew they might be hesitant to meet if they had any indication that the meeting would be lengthy.

After making the appointment, my follow-up email would restate that I would take no more than thirty minutes of the prospect's time.

When the actual meeting took place, I noted the time at the beginning and then paused at the thirty-minute mark, thanking the prospect for the time and suggesting we conclude. In many cases, the prospect would indicate

> Remember these three tips in getting ready for the visit:
>
> ◆ Honor/respect the time commitment.
>
> ◆ Take note of interests.
>
> ◆ Use names/references.
>
> **principle**

that we could continue and not worry about the time. The key is that I paid attention to, and honored, my promise. You simply have to play by the rules.

Pay Attention to Prospects' Interests

If prospects mention something about their children, their pets, their hobbies—anything important to them—when you first connect, you'd darn well better remember it!

So, let's say that during your initial phone conversation, the prospect mentions her daughter Susan has a big soccer tournament coming up. First, remember the daughter's name and, second, ask how the tournament went when you meet face to face. There's a good chance your prospect has already forgotten about the event but will be impressed that you took note and asked about it.

Showing that you are attentive to what is important to the prospect is critical, especially at this early stage. To make sure these little details don't slip my mind, I often record these anecdotes using a portable audio recorder immediately after the visit has concluded.

Drop Names

If you know someone who is acquainted with the prospect and have permission to mention that person's name, by all means, do so. In higher education, a favorite method of mine has been to get to know highly regarded emeriti faculty members and ask them about some of their favorite students with whom they still stay in touch. These former students are typically doing well in their professional careers and are glad to meet with me to hear how Dr. Smith is doing as well as to learn what's new on campus. On occasion, I have even met faculty members so highly regarded that their former students decided to create endowment funds in their mentors' names.

Saving a Tree

When preparing for the call, should you assemble printed materials that will supplement your visit?

Perhaps, but don't overdo it.

As a new development officer, I thought I should bring along every newsletter, brochure, and magazine outlining the merits of our organization that I could get my hands on. The more, the better. Right?

Well, guess what? Most of your prospects are too busy to read all that stuff! You run the risk of overwhelming your prospects.

In addition to my work as a development officer, I have also supported major gifts in a communications role. As part of this work, I created written material intended to be used for qualification visits. One time, after I created a multiple-page brochure, a veteran fundraiser confided to me, "It looks nice, but I really can't use anything longer than one page. My prospects will look at a single page, but that's it."

My colleague was right. People, especially highly successful people, have only a limited amount of time and energy available for even the

---

Offering Valuable Information

When I worked for the American Red Cross, I made personal visits with some of our donors who had made direct-mail (annual) gifts to support disaster relief. For the visits, I often took along statistics from our local Red Cross chapter describing how many people we had helped during the previous year. Since house fires were typically the most common local disaster response, my data might include how many people we had provided emergency housing for, how many meals we had provided, and similar data. Such information was almost always well received and appreciated.

Example

very best fundraisers. As a result, we need to summarize and get to the point.

Eventually, I became adept at putting together one-page (two-sided) highlights that have proven to be helpful for our development officers. They provide a snapshot of the college, department, or program that the fundraiser represents, providing just enough detail to pique the prospect's interests.

A sample of this work can be seen in **Appendix B.** Please note that the front of the College of Health and Human Services document includes contact information and key statistics, while the back (second page) includes notable facts or "bragging points."

Location, Location, Location

Where is the best place to conduct the qualification call? Office? Home? Neutral location (restaurant, coffee shop, etc.)? Your organization?

The short answer to this question is wherever the prospect will meet you. Let's face it, if the prospect is providing you with the opportunity to visit, you should meet at a location of the prospect's choosing.

I've had colleagues tell me they don't like to meet prospects in their offices, mainly because they can be easily interrupted with pressing phone calls, projects, etc. I have absolutely no problem meeting at the prospect's office. If you find that the prospect's attention is divided there, deal with it and attempt to schedule a follow-up meeting in a less hectic environment. Many prospects I meet with schedule an office conference room where interruption is less likely.

Restaurants and coffee shops can be a bit more casual, but there is often a noise factor you cannot control, and the chances of being interrupted there are often greater than in a more sterile office environment. You can ask the server not to interrupt you, but there are still other variables (loud conversations, babies crying, etc.) that can cause difficulty in a public setting.

I believe meeting in a prospect's home is quite ideal. Your prospect is most likely to be relaxed and more open at home, so definitely take advantage of this opportunity if presented. The downside is that if you are invited into the home, your time commitment is likely to be longer. If you are expecting to make two or three visits in a day while traveling, home visits can throw you off your schedule. Plan accordingly depending on the location of your calls.

A Day in the Life of a Major Gift Officer

I'm often asked, "How many discovery calls can I make in a day?"

It depends. If you are making visits within a relatively small geographic area, it should not be difficult to make three visits in one day, allowing for drive time, traffic, and other variables.

As an example, at one time I regularly traveled to Southern California to make visits with WMU alumni and friends. We have quite a few constituents there, so it wasn't hard to find enough potential prospects. The problem with the area, as those of us who have spent time there know, is that it can be a long drive between destinations. Furthermore, even shorter drives are frequently delayed by traffic. So, sometimes I could make only two visits in a day. If they were two good visits, my time spent was still worth it.

As a rule of thumb, I tried to leave at least a one-hour "pad" between visits. So, if I had a 9:00 a.m. visit and an hour drive to my next appointment, I would not schedule the second visit earlier than noon. Using the same principle, I would schedule the third visit for mid to late afternoon. Between visits, I would type or make an audio recording of my call report (debrief) from the previous meeting and then prepare/review notes pertaining to my next meeting.

Here's what a daily schedule might look like:

8:30 a.m.: drive to first appointment.

9:00 to 10:00 a.m.: visit with prospect one.

10:00 to 11:00 a.m.: drive to next appointment.

11:00 a.m. to noon: arrive for second appointment; debrief from first meeting; prepare for second meeting.

Noon to 1:30 p.m.: visit with prospect two.

1:30 to 2:30 p.m.: drive to third appointment.

2:30 to 4:00 p.m.: arrive for third meeting; debrief and prepare.

4:00 to 5:00 p.m.: visit with prospect three.

5:00 p.m.: drive back to hotel; debrief.

This is just one example. You might find your prospects prefer meetings after work or at dinner get-togethers, which is fine. The point is that if you structure your day accordingly, you can accomplish a great deal without feeling overly rushed. Many times, I found that I could file my call or trip reports describing the interactions between visits. If you follow this strategy, you are more likely to recall many of the details of the meetings.

I like the on-the-go call report technique because you avoid an exhaustive brain dump at the end of the day. In turn, that allows you more time to relax and get ready for the next day of visits.

I will admit that I am not the greatest road warrior, but I could keep this schedule up for a workweek. So, when I traveled to Southern California, my goal would be to make fifteen visits, or three per day, over a total of five days. I often encountered at least one day in that span where someone was a no-show, or when three visits were logistically impossible, but thirteen or fourteen visits in a week is still quite productive.

Meeting at Your Organization

I think it's more difficult to persuade the prospect to visit your organization for the first visit, but I have seen some do it successfully. It works best when your CEO or key volunteer invites the prospect to the nonprofit for lunch and a tour. Again, this is a greater commitment of time and resources than the typical office visit, so you want to have some idea that the prospect has potential.

In the end, there is no right or wrong location in which to conduct a qualification call, but it is good to think about the advantages and disadvantages of potential sites as you determine your strategy.

To Recap

◆ The impression you make is of utmost importance.

◆ Prepare thoughtfully for each visit.

◆ The right location is wherever the prospect will meet you.

◆ Try for three face-to-face visits daily.

Chapter Eight

The Visit

IN THIS CHAPTER

- ···→ Your objectives

- ···→ Being enthusiastic

- ···→ Scripting and conducting the visit

- ···→ Casual but purposeful

Now we're going to delve into the meat of the topic. What do you say and do to make sure the initial meeting is a success?

This is a good time to think about what it is you would like to achieve and what you might like to have happen when the meeting is concluded.

At a minimum, you want to determine how interested a prospect is in your organization and, given appropriate cultivation steps, if the prospect might be likely to consider a significant investment in your organization.

You want to know the prospect's connections to your organization. Is the prospect an alumnus (education) or a grateful patient (health care)? Has the prospect, or a loved one, received services from your organization (human service, i.e., Red Cross)? Does the prospect know anyone on your board of directors or on your staff?

What is the prospect's impression of your organization? If it is not favorable, are there ways to address these concerns? Does the prospect think your work is important? If so, why?

As great as all of these questions are, there is one data point that tops all others. Does this person have the capacity to give? It sounds simple, but if the prospect does not have the money, that's it. You're done. Cross this one off your list.

Of course, you can't truly understand the issue of capacity until you get to know your prospect. Even publicly available prospect data, i.e., the approximate value of the individual's house, needs to be verified. All of the various life situations that can affect the giving decision must be explored. If a prospect has three children currently in college, a major gift in the near future is probably not likely. A divorce, the death of a loved one, a recent

---

The Numbers Game

Earlier, I mentioned that as many as half of the individuals you have targeted for discovery visits will not meet with you. I'm sorry to tell you that the odds for a major gift from those who will meet with you are not any better. That's why you need to be regimented in your approach. Let's say you have identified one hundred people who should be qualified. We know that typically only fifty might meet with you.

So, let's say that over the course of a year, you make fifty discovery calls. That's around four a month, certainly doable if you are working full time in major gifts. (If you are working part time in major gifts, try for a more modest goal—perhaps two a month.) What I am suggesting is that no more than half (twenty-five) of those visits will yield a prospect that you will want to move forward for cultivation and, eventually, solicitation.

The bottom line is, you have to see people, and you must be disciplined in assessing who might really be a good prospect. Don't fill up your portfolio with folks who will probably not make major gifts. Be brutally honest when you are sizing up your list.

If that sounds discouraging, don't worry about it. If you do your homework and stay focused, I believe that eventually you will be successful. Just remember that you are probably going to meet a number of people you will really enjoy but who are not going to give. Cross them off, because you are also going to meet people you will enjoy and who will give generously. Some will even thank you for the opportunity.

business merger, or an upcoming retirement are other factors that could impact the gift decision.

Above all, the major gift qualification call needs to be both strategic and purposeful. You need to approach your visits from a sales perspective and understand from the beginning that a good number of your visits will not lead to major gifts. That means you need to make a lot of visits and cross off the prospects who do not show potential.

(Do Not) Curb Your Enthusiasm

The energy you project when conducting qualification calls makes a huge difference. In my circumstance, I remind myself before reaching out to someone new that I'm very proud of the university I work for. I enjoy telling our alumni and friends about the exciting things that are happening on campus.

Just thinking about the fact that my university is a great place with great people puts me in an excellent frame of mind. I believe most of the prospects I meet can sense my excitement and enjoy engaging with me because of it.

While it is important to be respectful of people's time, often the best fundraisers are those who naturally assume that the people they call will want to meet with them and will benefit from the opportunity of the visit. Development officers should never apologize for who they are or feel like they are creating an imposition by asking for a meeting. Fundraisers who treat the request like an inconvenience are not successful.

What I'm saying is, if you are confident in yourself and proud of the organization you work for, don't be shy. I promise you, your enthusiasm will be contagious.

The Casual but Purposeful Visit

I have a little phrase I used to say to myself when arriving for a visit with a new prospective donor. The mantra "casual but purposeful" has served me well over the years.

To explain, I have found that the most productive ID calls occur when I can speak in a relaxed and relatively informal manner. Even though you need to have a sales orientation, I believe that fundraising visits must also be relatively low-key. People have a hard time finding their passion—a critical factor in giving—when they feel stressed or rushed.

One of my favorite donors in the WMU College of Education once told me, "I'd love to meet with you, but I don't want to be rushed." He wanted our visit to be a relaxed and social one.

Accordingly, after our relationship continued at a leisurely pace, he made both an outright major gift and a planned/estate gift commitment. It was important that I gave him the time and space to make a gift that was personally fulfilling.

While a casual tone in the first visit is helpful, I believe you still need to maintain focus and be strategic. You definitely want to establish a relaxed tone but, at the same time, your prospect should never have the thought that you might be wasting valuable time. There needs to be a sense of purpose.

A good way to establish such focus is to set expectations at the beginning of the visit. So, let's say I have been given thirty minutes for the meeting. At the start, I'll thank the prospect for the time invested in our meeting and ask if we can talk a while about the prospect's interests and how perhaps those interests might intersect with my organization.

In other words, I want to see if there is a connection and a possible mutual interest (which might lead to a gift opportunity). I will also ask the prospect at the beginning if we can agree to pause toward the end of our time, perhaps a few minutes before we conclude. The wrap-up discussion will explore next steps or what follow-up action will occur.

Why do I say this at the beginning? I have found that some people appear, at first, a bit confused (or even nervous) about my purpose and what I am expecting of them. Often taking the simple step of clarifying what might or might not occur as a result of the meeting brings relief to the prospect. Typically, the individual relaxes and becomes more comfortable once a potential road map has been laid out.

Depending on your style, experience, and comfort level, the preceding advice may be all you really need to conduct a successful qualification call. However, if you are a novice fundraiser, I believe you need a little more structure. Never fear. I have a model that works for those just dipping their toes into major gift work.

Scripting the Visit

If you will recall the letter provided in Chapter Four (my dean in the College of Education introducing me), it is easy to format a visit that logically follows this lead. You might remember that the dean's letter mentions my desire to "determine perceptions and solicit input." I believe it is important to approach this task in a very systematic way. In fact, when I was first getting started, I actually took a list of questions into my meetings and wrote down the responses.

When using this method, I took time to assure my prospects that their answers were absolutely confidential and would be shared internally only (i.e., with my dean) to determine how we could improve our programs and services. Of the more than one hundred discovery calls I conducted using the written list of questions, I can recall only three

---

The Lungo Viaggio

I recently returned from a great experience at a fundraising conference held in northern Italy. I was honored to present at the Festival del Fundraising, where I met many students studying in the master of fundraising program at the University of Bologna. One of them taught me the Italian traveling phrase "lungo viaggio," which means "long journey."

Lungo viaggio is a good descriptor for my personal approach when making major gift qualification calls. I start my visit by telling my prospect that I hope our discussion will be the beginning of a mutually fulfilling journey. I really don't have a specific expectation at the outset. I'm simply inviting the prospect to join me in heading in an agreed-upon direction. Again, I'm telling the prospect that I don't have a preset agenda and that I want the prospect to feel free to depart from our journey at any time.

---

occasions when the interviewee appeared to be uneasy with my recording the answers. In those cases, I "winged" it, putting the questions away and conducting the interview informally. Eventually, as I became more polished, I didn't need the written list and conducted all of my discovery calls this way.

Why might a list of questions, rather than a free-form interview, be a good idea? Primarily because the qualification call should place focus on listening to the prospect. I found that when I departed from my discovery call questions, I tended to talk too much. To properly qualify our donors, we must invite them to tell their story. After they have done so, there will be plenty of opportunity to make our case for giving.

Discovery Call Questions

Here are some sample questions you can use in the course of a structured identification call/interview. Think of these in terms of "mix and match." Not every question will be suitable for your nonprofit.

1. **What are your impressions of our organization? What are its strengths and weaknesses?**
This allows the prospect to provide advice and insight. Acknowledge and thank the prospect for both positive and negative feedback.

2. **How does our nonprofit compare with other institutions offering similar programs?**
For this question, ask the prospect to think in terms of your standing among nonprofits that deliver similar or identical services.

3. **How has our organization helped in your career?**
This is a great question for any nonprofit whose constituents gain skills applicable to professional careers.

4. **Do you receive our publications (newsletters)? What are your impressions of these? What topics would you like to know more about?**
The answer provides clues about how closely the prospect is engaged with your work. More importantly, it gives great insight about where interest might center regarding a gift opportunity.

5. **(If prospect is a financial contributor) *Thank you!* Why do you support our organization? Are there particular services we provide/things about our mission that motivate you to give?**
This helps define donors' priorities for possible future gift opportunities.

6. **What do you feel are the top priorities for which our organization should seek financial support?**
Some prospects will not have a ready answer for this because they haven't given the matter a great deal of thought. Others, however, will have specific ideas, and some will even share their thoughts about philanthropy in general. The latter tend to be individuals who are comfortable with giving and, other factors being equal, are often the best prospects.

7. **Would *you* consider financially supporting these priorities?**
This question equates to "asking without really asking." Often, prospects will respond that they might. In the event a prospect hesitates in responding, I indicate that for the purposes of this meeting, I am merely trying to learn about the potential interests of our constituents. In no way should the question be considered a formal request or proposal, as that would be inappropriate for a first meeting.

8. **Would you be willing, in some fashion, to serve as a volunteer for our organization in our efforts to attract private support?**
This can be used by nonprofits seeking to engage constituents in their fundraising efforts. Perhaps you have created or are considering creating a development committee or are simply looking for volunteers to review your organization's case for support. If so, use the discovery call to supplement these efforts. If not, skip the question so you don't set up any false expectations.

9. **Can you name three friends/colleagues who might like to learn more about our organization or who might also be interested in serving as volunteers?**
This question can assist you in keeping the donor pipeline filled. Make sure if you ask this question that you do attempt to follow up with the referred individuals. Not only will following up bring potential new prospects, but it will also help you build credibility with the prospect who referred you. When you follow up on such referrals, it's only a matter of time before your original prospect hears about it. You have provided evidence to that prospect that you were listening and are taking the person's advice seriously.

These questions have served me well, but I don't claim that they will be perfectly suited for every development officer. My central point is that structure—in this case, a list of questions—can be very helpful not only to fledgling fundraisers but also to organizations trying to ramp up or reinvigorate their major gift programs. The qualification call is a much more manageable task when a system is in place to guide the process. Using these questions, or similar ones, you should be able to reasonably determine if your prospects have potential for future major gifts.

Closing the Visit

At the conclusion of a question-and-answer session, after thanking the prospect for participating, it is a good time to pause and discuss potential next steps. The discussion might sound something like this:

"Mrs. Smith, thank you so much for taking the time to answer my questions so thoughtfully. I was particularly intrigued to hear about your interest in (name of program) and wondered if you would like to learn more about it. I'm planning to be back in town next month and would like to bring you some additional information. Do you think we could find a convenient time to get together?"

If at all possible, I like to schedule the next meeting right then and there. If you can, you'll save yourself quite a bit of time devoted to telephone tag and email exchanges.

In Chapter Ten, we'll further discuss setting up and conducting the follow-up meeting.

If you are ready and raring to start making discovery calls at this point, please do yourself a favor and read the next chapter first. It provides advice about how you will use the information gathered through the discovery call questions.

To Recap

- ◆ Use a list of set questions to qualify your prospects.

- ◆ Conduct the visit in a casual, purposeful manner.

- ◆ Conclude your visit with a concrete next step.

Chapter Nine

After the Visit

Any good fundraising operation uses some type of report or form that documents the information gained from each donor visit. Most commonly, it is referred to as a call report or trip report.

My rule of thumb for call reports is to either type them out or make an audio recording of my report on the same day the visit occurs. When I was I traveling a lot and making three calls daily, it did make for long days, but it was worth it. By the next morning, I would have forgotten some of the nuances of the visits.

For qualification visits, I like to use a specialized version of the call report. It contains an inventory list designed to help me debrief after the meeting.

Unlike the discovery call questions, the inventory list is not directly referred to during the actual call. I do, however, like to review the list immediately before each discovery call so I can frame the visit in a way that will help me fill out the list effectively.

The inventory list can be used as a stand-alone document, or it can be incorporated into the nonprofit's standard call report.

Discovery Call Inventory

Here's a list of indicators that can be used as a guide when filling out the discovery call report. Many of these indicators can be answered using responses to the discovery call questions.

I always try to review the list just before I meet with a new prospect so I can be ready to provide responses after the call ends.

1. **Prospect's relationship with our organization**
   Is the prospect highly engaged in our work, minimally engaged, or not engaged at all?

2. **Prospect's perception, opinion, and/or attitude regarding our organization**
   How does the prospect personally feel about our organization? Make a list of all likes and dislikes.

3. **Prospect's sense of our organization's needs (with priorities indicated)**
   See question number six in discovery call questions.

4. **Indications of financial capacity**
   What type of vehicle does the prospect drive? What are the prospect's hobbies? Where does the prospect go on vacation?

5. **Likelihood the prospect could become a significant annual fund donor**
   Often verified by prospect's gift history, if any. An assessment of the prospect's inclination to give on a long-term, ongoing basis.

6. **Likelihood the prospect could become a planned gift donor**
   A continuation of the previous question about annual giving. Also shaped by family situation. If you learn during the discovery call that the prospect has no children/heirs, this might be a positive indicator for a planned gift.

7. **Likelihood the prospect could become a major (outright) gift donor**
   Indicated not only by the prospect's relationship with the organization but also by life events (recent promotion, children in college, etc.).

When using this list, aim to be as concise as possible in your responses, providing no more than one or two short sentences. When you are qualifying a significant number of individuals, brevity is helpful for strategic purposes. You need to be able to review all of your inventories easily and then decide who your top-priority prospects should be for follow-up.

The discovery call inventory can be inserted into the overall call report, which should also include a general summary of the meeting and what was discussed as well as the plan for what should occur next. The plan should include specific tasks and due dates for each. Tasks might include:

1. By (date), send thank-you note.

2. By (date), send resource materials relating to discussion.

3. By (date), schedule follow-up meeting.

The first task, the thank-you note, should always be on your list. Even if your qualification call determines that the prospect should not be cultivated, you must thank the prospect for the meeting. Not only is it the right thing to do, but if you don't say thank you, the word may get out. As fundraisers, our reputation is everything. If we are perceived as being less than courteous, we're doomed.

I recommend that your thank-you notes be as personal in nature as possible. I like to include a specific reference to something that was discussed during the meeting. I think handwritten notes are great, but I have to confess that my handwriting is not great. I print out my thank-you notes on business letterhead, but I always make it a point to sign them by hand, and I often include a short, personal, handwritten note on the letter. I also avoid the postage meter and use an actual stamp. It's easy to do, and the additional personalization will help you stand out.

Please refer to the thank-you letter located in **Appendix C** as an example. This was an actual thank-you note I sent, with the name changed. I remember this particular gentleman was interested in law school opportunities for our students, hence my reference. You may also notice I provided him with an opportunity to come back to campus in a formal setting (invited speaker) or more informally (he can call me on short notice).

If you do it right, the post-visit note will be just the first in a series of expressions of gratitude as your relationship with your prospect continues and grows. For example, saying thank you should be at the top of your agenda during your next meeting.

A further discussion of next steps, including conducting the follow-up meeting, is on deck in the next chapter.

To Recap

◆ Write your call report immediately.

◆ A list of questions can help you prioritize prospects.

◆ Stand out with a thoughtful thank-you note.

Chapter Ten

Following Up

IN THIS CHAPTER

···→ Creating the cultivation plan

···→ Your strategy for success

···→ Setting up the next meeting

···→ Being realistic

···→ The prospect team

···→ Agenda/who to bring

The beauty of the qualification call is that it should really give you all of the information needed to set up the second meeting. Your prospect has told you a great deal about personal history and interests. As a development officer, it is your job to serve those interests.

As you consider a cultivation plan for your prospect, I believe it is a good idea to think about a road map. After the qualification call, you should not only be thinking about your next step, but you should also consider what might happen during a third step—and beyond.

Let's go back to the example of Mrs. Smith. As promised, you returned to her town and enjoyed a very nice lunch meeting, during which you delved into the program of her interest.

My "Typical" Strategy

Using my College of Education background as an example, let's say that Mrs. Smith is a retired teacher. She's really interested in our internship program, so during our next meeting, I bring her a brochure with information about our teaching interns that contains testimonials from our students. I tell Mrs. Smith that we are developing new resources that help our students excel during the practice teaching experience. She's intrigued. That leads to a third meeting on our campus where Mrs. Smith meets our intern coordinator and some of our current students.

This was a script I followed with some success a number of times. If I could predict how the second visit might go, I would naturally begin thinking about what a third step might entail.

I should also note that by following this script, the prospect was often ready to be solicited for a gift soon after the third meeting, perhaps during the fourth or fifth visit.

Paralysis by Analysis

I think it is great to map out a multifaceted strategy for a donor. I have to say, though, that on many occasions, I have seen this approach backfire. While you need to be thoughtful and purposeful in setting out your cultivation plan, it can be tempting to overdo it. Paralysis by analysis, if you will. Some development officers are more comfortable spending their time mapping out a plan to the point that they never getting around to executing it. A better idea is a little strategy and a lot of donor interaction.

I try to think about what the next step might be after the one I am currently undertaking and, if possible, what the ultimate goal might be. I might have a prospect who I think may consider creating a scholarship with a $25,000 gift. Sometime later, I might change my mind and ask her for $500,000 to endow a faculty research fund.

My point? Don't worry so much about plotting the exact path. Just have a goal in mind (which may change), and keep working toward that goal. At the end of the day, does it really matter how you got there?

Following Up

As you plan your follow-up meeting, try again to put yourself in your prospect's shoes. If you can, answer these questions:

What Does the Prospect Want to Know?

Your discovery call questions should provide some answers to this question. If you have an indication of the prospect's interests, you can certainly provide the appropriate information. I found that after doing a number of discovery calls, I became fairly adept at figuring out what the prospect might want to know even without the prospect specifically telling me. The ability to anticipate unasked questions is a skill that all accomplished fundraisers eventually learn. Prospective donors are impressed when someone "reads their mind" in this way.

Who Can Best Tell the Story?

Perhaps you have determined for the follow-up meeting that it would be a good idea to bring in someone from your organization who is an expert in the prospect's area of interest. During my Red Cross days, I was often able to bring one of our disaster-response volunteers along on a donor call. It's a great idea to provide access to frontline personnel so your supporters can speak directly to those who are putting their gifts to work.

What Information/Interaction Would Best Serve the Prospect's Needs?

In answering this question, I try to consider both the prospect's interests and personality type. It makes sense to provide some level of detail (evaluation reports, budget data, etc.) to individuals who are more quiet and analytical in nature. For prospects who are more socially inclined, an event invitation might be a good choice. For prospects who appear to be engaged in or are passionate about your mission, think about bringing along someone who is a direct recipient of charitable giving. For those of us in higher education, that might be a student who is a scholarship recipient.

Follow-up meetings can be a lot of fun. You can be very creative in building the new relationship with your prospect. At the same time, however, you still have to be pragmatic in your approach.

As we have previously discussed, you have to have a strategy. Taking that one step farther, you also have to be both realistic and purposeful.

Let's Get Real

The ability to be truly realistic is one of the greatest talents a development officer can master. Idealism often reigns (for good reason) in the nonprofit world, and as fundraisers, we must express that sense of optimism in our daily work. We must simultaneously, however, walk the tightrope of being the voice of reason.

It's critical to maintain a sense of realism as we create a sustainable donor plan. Such a plan requires that we objectively answer key cultivation questions.

For example, how quickly should we be moving the prospect along? If we are overly optimistic, it may be tempting to speed up the cultivation to a rate that is uncomfortable for the prospect. If that sounds like you, flip the script and put yourself in the prospect's place. How would you feel if you were being engaged at this pace?

To be purposeful, we must keep our goals, and the goals of our prospect, in constant focus. How does the follow-up visit move us logically forward toward the goal of a major gift? Does the prospect see value in the interaction being planned? Are you and the prospect of a common mind that you are working toward an outcome that will be mutually fulfilling?

In considering the location for the next meeting, refer back to your strategy and what the prospect wants to know. I find the second meeting can be a great time to bring the prospect to where your nonprofit operates. If the prospect wants to know more about your work, doesn't it make sense to invite the prospect to where the work is being done?

The good news is that if you have conducted the qualification call well, your prospect is likely to be much more flexible regarding the location of the next meeting. If you have captured the prospect's attention, this individual will be much more likely to follow your suggestion.

The Prospect Team

It's also important to note that the follow-up meeting is a time to invite the prospect's partner or spouse to participate. Practically every major gift decision is made only after the prospect's significant other is consulted. For that reason, some of my fundraising colleagues have told me that they always try to involve the spouse/partner in the introductory meeting. While I think there is some merit to that approach, it's really not that simple.

Personally, I haven't had great success with that endeavor. I find many of the best prospects have busy schedules that make it difficult enough just trying to meet with them solo. When you push to include both partners in the first meeting, the chance to get together often falls apart. It does so not only because of schedules but also because you as the fundraiser have not yet made a positive, in-person impression. I have found it much more productive to "win over" my primary prospect during the qualification call and then invite the prospect's spouse/partner for the second meeting.

Because it is important to include everyone who might influence donor decisions, you need to ask about family connections during the qualification meeting. I try to learn not only who the prospect's partner is, but I also try to find out some of the partner's interests. Children can certainly influence donor decisions, so it is good to learn about them as well.

Here's an example of a strategy I have found to be effective. Let's say I qualify Mrs. Jones and find her to be a good prospect. It turns out that Mrs. Jones and I are both big football fans, so my initial inclination is to invite her to campus for homecoming weekend and center our activities around the football game. However, I learn that her husband, Mr. Jones, doesn't care much for sports at all. He would probably come to the homecoming game, but he might not have a good time.

Mrs. Jones tells me that her husband's true passion is the fine arts. He's an avid theatergoer and music aficionado. I might then suggest to Mrs. Jones that she and her husband join me on campus for a Gold Company (our award-winning vocal performance group) concert, followed by a play in our Dalton Theatre.

By making such an offer, I'm showing that I am thinking of Mrs. Jones' desire to make her husband happy. She, in turn, is delighted that he winds up having a great time. And now that Mr. Jones thinks I'm a decent fellow, he'll be much more likely to join his wife when I invite the two of them to be my guests at a future gridiron contest.

The Cultivation Team

Although we touched on it a bit previously, let's discuss further who (if anyone) you might bring with you from your organization to meet with the prospect during the second meeting.

In my initial years of major gifts work, I tended to default to introducing the prospect to the highest-ranking official within my organization. After a while, though, I figured out that my CEO or university president might not always be the right person for the follow-up meeting. Instead, the prospect might better enjoy meeting a student, a volunteer direct-service provider, or someone else who could be closely connected to the prospect's interests.

Here's an example from my work. In 2008, Western Michigan University started an initiative that helps individuals who are transitioning out of the foster-care system gain access to college. Historically, very few foster youth (less than 3 percent of the total group) have been able to earn college degrees. But our "Fostering Success" program has turned the numbers around, featuring a freshman- to sophomore-year student retention rate of 75 percent to date.

The Outsider Who Is Really an Insider

When scheduling follow-up meetings with your prospects, you don't have to limit yourself to introducing someone from your organization. Someone who is not formally affiliated could be your best choice.

observation

In searching for private funding to sustain our program, I contacted a local family foundation that I thought might have an interest. As I talked with the foundation, I realized that I needed someone who could really tell the story of our foster youth.

I was able to recruit a WMU alumnus who was a product of the foster care system for this task. Other than being an alum, this individual had no other formal affiliation to our foster youth program or the university. At the same time, this gentleman's personal story—the struggles he faced as a college student—actually provided the inspiration for the initiative.

In the end, the alumnus accompanied me on a personal visit to the foundation, and the meeting was a big hit. The result was a major gift that has propelled our program to its current success. In fact, not only is our program enjoying great triumphs, but we also are now training other colleges and universities around the state of Michigan to set up similar programs a mere four years after our program started.

Just remember that you don't have to limit your thinking when scheduling the follow-up meeting. Be bold. Don't be afraid to do something different. You might just find that the best person to bring to the table is someone from the outside. If someone else can best tell your story, invite that person in.

To Recap

◆ Create a road map for cultivating your prospect.

◆ Don't overthink your strategy.

◆ Anticipate the prospect's unasked questions.

◆ Consider both the prospect team and the fundraising team.

Chapter Eleven

Trends and Topics

IN THIS CHAPTER

···→ Generational considerations

···→ Considering various nonprofit sectors

···→ Future trends

Will the strategies I have outlined here work for every prospective major donor in your fundraising portfolio?

Of course not!

The techniques, however, will work for the majority of the individuals who have the capacity and interest to make a major investment in your organization's work. They have been tested across multiple nonprofit sectors with major gift prospects from every imaginable life circumstance.

It is generally believed that the best major gift prospects tend to be forty years of age or older, with an optimum age demographic of fifty to sixty-five. This age range has proven to be the most fruitful in my personal experience as a major gift officer. If you have a strong planned giving emphasis in your development program, the top age may be older than fifty to sixty-five, perhaps as old as seventy-five.

My point here—although there can be exceptions—is that your current major donor pool is likely to have very few, if any, individuals in their twenties or thirties. That's a good thing for you (and me), because some of my strategies won't work for this younger age group.

I have several nephews and nieces who fit this demographic. I can tell you from personal experience that phoning them, or even emailing them, will often result in either a delayed response or no response at all.

So, how do I get their attention? Send text messages to their cell phones, of course!

You may remember in Chapter Four, I wrote that I was personally opposed to sending a prospect a text message as an icebreaker. See the problem here?

With this in mind, it's entirely possible that within a generation, some of my outreach methods will be obsolete. In the meantime, we are all forced to deal with the fact that the phone call is one of the best ways to make contact with a prospective major gift donor.

Strategies for Various Nonprofit Sectors

It is true that some sectors in the nonprofit arena offer more consistent and natural connections than others. Higher education, where I work, certainly does provide the advantage of having alumni as potential donors. There is also an expectation among some alumni, especially wealthy ones, that their alma mater will try to reach out and cultivate them.

I will say that sometimes the connections offered by colleges and universities are overrated. At many leading higher-education institutions, giving from non-alumni, or "friends" of the university, is increasing at a higher rate than giving from the alumni population. This tells me that, while having potential donors who have a natural connection to your organization may be helpful, the factor does not necessarily guarantee success. The big money is going to colleges that excel in building relationships with *all* interested high-potential donors.

Religious organizations may have an even greater built-in constituency that allows them to raise tons of money. However, much of the giving comes from consistent weekly giving rather than one-time major gifts.

Hospitals and other health care institutions also benefit from a constituency of the "grateful patient." My colleagues in health care fundraising have indicated both the positives and challenges of this group. Although typically unfounded, concerns occasionally arise that somehow development officers may be trying to take advantage of individuals who are vulnerable. I don't believe this is a major problem, but it is something to be mindful of.

Other sectors are more challenged in this area. While human service charities addressing the needs of the disadvantaged, such as homeless shelters and soup kitchens, have a compelling mission, these nonprofits are sometimes affected by a lack of donor retention. People see a need in their community and try to help, but if there is no systematic measure of follow-up and engagement (which is, unfortunately, too frequent an occurrence), their contributions are often "one and done."

Volunteer involvement and connections become more and more important in fundraising efforts for charities with fewer natural constituencies. This group can often provide access to donors with ability and inclination because of their unique insider perspective.

Nonprofits with donor databases filled with individuals who may have little direct involvement (as was the case for me at the Red Cross) need to redouble their efforts in cultivation and retention. Much of this can be done without labor-intensive, face-to-face contact. Direct mail and electronic communication stewardship can help cultivate donors to the point that they may one day consider a major gift. However, as this book describes, a major gift rarely occurs with this ongoing "soft" cultivation alone. At some point, the donor must be qualified, in person, and eventually *asked* for a significant gift.

Future Trends

My crystal ball tells me that face-to-face qualification will continue to be critical to the major gifts process for many, many years to come. There are several factors, however, that may affect how we plan our donor qualification strategies in the future.

Electronic Giving and Communication

Most recent estimates indicate that online giving is rising but is still not a dominant factor in philanthropy. The proliferation of technology, however, cannot be overlooked. Of course, we must seek and capture all bits of available electronic information, including email addresses, Twitter handles, and other data to connect with our donors. The key for nonprofits is their ability to segment their major donor/prospect databases electronically in much the same way they have segmented direct-mail appeal lists. For example, certain higher-level prospects may be included in a small group of individuals who receive "exclusive" or "insider's" messages from the nonprofit board chair or CEO. Interaction at this elite level can result in closer connections and personal visits with fundraisers and top charity personnel.

Electronic communication will also have a larger presence in cultivation and stewardship after the ID visit. I know several major gift officers who effectively use communication tools such as Skype to facilitate donor relationship building when personal visits are impractical due to distance. While such online video chats can be very helpful in the moves management process, in my opinion, they will never replace the face-to-face qualification and solicitation of prospects.

Special Events

The days of the nonprofit annual meeting may be dwindling. Instead of holding a large event because the organization has always held one in the past, there will be a shift to creating smaller personalized events with specific agendas. For example, if many of your major donors, or prospective major donors, do not play golf, should you really conduct an annual golf outing? Isn't it better to get to know your major donor/prospect population to learn about their interests? Maybe they are more likely to attend a special theater event instead of coming to the president's suite at a football game.

These will be among the strategic hallmarks of future special events:

◆ To the greatest extent possible, the potential interests of prospects will be determined, and special events will be designed accordingly. This may be done through qualification visits, surveys, volunteer recommendations, and other inputs.

◆ Personal invitations to events will be extended for prospective donors with the highest potential. This will primarily be a staff-driven endeavor.

◆ Events will increasingly facilitate the introduction of prospects to high-level nonprofit officials/VIPs.

◆ Events will be systematically employed to foster future face-to-face qualification meetings. Following events, development personnel will reach out to prospects to determine their impressions of the festivities and to formally qualify them as potential major gift donors.

Competition for Major Donors

With major government cuts to reduce the federal deficit looming, more and more nonprofits are either starting new major gift programs or bolstering existing ones. The nonprofits that are best at building meaningful interactions with potential benefactors will be the ones that will best mitigate the dire prospect of federal and state budget cutting.

The increasing professionalism of fundraising will also create congestion in the pursuit of major gifts. Years ago, many considered fundraising to be an accidental profession, meaning individuals who began fundraising did so out of necessity and often with little or no formal training. Today, there are a myriad of credentialing programs and an increasing number of higher-education certificate and formal degree programs for fundraisers.

Just a decade ago, I was among a relatively small number of individuals with both a fundraising credential (Certified Fund Raising Executive, or CFRE) and a degree in fundraising (MA in philanthropy development, Saint Mary's [Minnesota] University). Today, there are considerably more who have completed such development training programs.

What all of this means is that more and more nonprofits are staffed by knowledgeable individuals who understand how to identify, cultivate, solicit, and steward donors who are capable of making major, and perhaps even transformational, investments. As a result, the competition for major donors is going to escalate.

As an example, there is a young woman currently working with me in foundation relations at WMU who is a recent college graduate. She has been active in nonprofit work for a number of years, and during her job interview, she told me she has a "secret passion for fundraising." I cannot imagine any of my peers making such a statement when I graduated from college some thirty years ago.

My advice to any charitable organization pondering a major gift effort is to get to it as soon as possible. Better to start today in building your inner circle of supporters than risk your nonprofit competitors beating you to the punch.

Increased Professionalism

I strongly believe the increasing professionalism of the fundraising field will continue to have a dramatic and positive impact on philanthropy. Further, I hope in some small way that this book contributes to the trend.

Given enough time, nonprofits that focus on the basics of donor identification and qualification will raise larger amounts of money compared with charities that do not. Additionally, nonprofits that excel in this task will raise money *faster* than their uncommitted counterparts.

Let me explain why. Using rigor in qualification calls, as explained in this book, will ultimately help nonprofits determine their best major gift prospects in a systematic and organized way. As such, they can better organize their efforts and be ready to solicit when the opportunity arises. I believe that many of today's nonprofits are simply not ready to ask when their donors are inclined to give. A real pity, it seems.

I also believe that nonprofits can effectively use qualification techniques to ask prospects for significant gifts, but perhaps not "mega-gifts," in a relatively short period of time.

As an example, let's say you have a prospect rated at $1 million in capacity for giving. The prospect likes your charity but unfortunately is not yet significantly engaged in your organization. You qualify the prospect and visit a few times. The prospect meets one of your volunteers and talks with a recipient of your work.

After that, you might sense (or, even better, the prospect will tell you) that the prospect would like to help. Despite the opportunity, you are probably not going to ask for $1 million because your donor is not yet a true insider.

So, what do you do? You ask for a "starter" gift, of course! Perhaps the prospect would consider a gift of $10,000, or $25,000, or even $50,000. I call such a gift a starter investment because the donor may be testing your organization to see that the money is well used.

Of course, you are grateful for the gift, and you do a great job of informing the donor of the gift's positive impact. When that happens, the donor then becomes a *real* stakeholder. When that happens, a larger or transformational gift may be feasible.

My point is that by being strategic and purposeful at the outset (with the discovery call), more philanthropic opportunities will eventually come to the forefront. Just remain patient and keep working hard.

To Recap

◆ Your best prospects will be between fifty and sixty-five years of age.

◆ Consider your charitable sector in determining strategy.

◆ Electronic communication and special events will play increasing roles in qualification and major gifts.

◆ Professionalism will make major gift work more competitive.

Chapter Twelve

Conclusion

In my years of experience as a major gift fundraiser, and as a colleague of fellow major gift officers, I have made a number of observations that relate to the task of qualifying donors.

Many development officers I have known just did not like to qualify donors. The experience was an unpleasant one for them. When they did try to reach out and make appointments with new prospects, they were usually not successful. As a result, they often fell into comfort zones, making multiple calls on prospects with lower gift capacities, many of whom were unlikely to ever make major gifts.

So, why did they keep seeing these people, you ask? Because they liked them, of course! In the end, however, they were not really helping their organization, and eventually they were forced to pursue another line of work.

Greenhoe's Fundraising Realities

Ever the pragmatist, I have formed a few opinions about fundraising and the potential of various individuals to make major gifts. In my opinion, prospects generally fall into one of three categories:

1. Prospects who will welcome your outreach, engage you meaningfully, and eventually agree to a significant investment that is mutually beneficial to them and to your nonprofit. In many cases, these "dream" prospects will even thank you for the opportunity!

2. Prospects who will not be interested in your work and do not wish to be engaged but who will do you the courtesy of telling you so. If that's the case, don't feel bad. That is totally part of the process. Cross them off your list. After all, there are plenty of other fish in the sea!

3. Prospects who will be happy to visit with you any time but really have no interest in a major gift. They love the social contact and are flattered by the attention, and they will take all of your time if you let them. Perhaps not intentionally, but they will even give you false hints that a major gift might be feasible. This is where tools like the discovery call questions in Chapter Eight will be helpful. If you set ground rules during the qualification call (i.e., asking if a prospect would potentially support a self-selected priority/program), you can, for the most part, avoid this potential "black hole" of major gift fundraising.

As wonderful as the development profession can be, we all have to remember that, in the end, it is about raising money. It has to be about results, not just activity.

principle

Being Resilient

Any fundraiser will have disappointing moments, especially those who are blazing a trail starting a new major gift effort. A great deal of patience, and some resilience, is needed to persevere.

One of the best ways to succeed is to develop a relationship with colleagues who may be facing some of the same issues you face. In my case, the pursuit of a master's degree in philanthropy and development has paid huge dividends. During the course of my studies at Saint Mary's (Minnesota) University, I developed close relationships with some very talented fundraisers. To this day, I feel I can call upon these colleagues and friends if I face a challenge with which I need help.

My college colleague example is just one of many potential resources, and as a fundraiser, you need to determine what support network works best for you. Maybe you can find such camaraderie, or even a mentor, through your local AFP chapter. Regardless of the source, when you talk regularly with fellow development colleagues, you'll often find someone who has faced the same challenge and has successfully addressed it.

Sharing Your Story

Many of the best fundraisers I know share two common traits. First, they are among the most optimistic people I know. Second, they exhibit an abundance of enthusiasm. These people are almost relentlessly positive and cheerful.

To be honest, I don't think either of these tendencies comes to me naturally, but I try to adopt these traits daily as a fundraiser. Fortunately for me, I absolutely love the university I work for. There's no question that my personal experience as a student at WMU—I loved my undergraduate days in Kalamazoo—have deeply influenced my unflagging enthusiasm as a university fundraiser.

One experience in particular continues to fuel my passion. Back in the early 1980s, I was a student in the WMU communications program. As an aspiring broadcaster (I did work a few years in radio early in my professional career), I took a number of courses centering on the television and media industry. One day during my junior year, I received a letter indicating that I had been selected as a recipient of the Fetzer Broadcasting

Scholarship. Fellow Michiganders no doubt know that the donor was the late John E. Fetzer, a former television and radio pioneer who at the time owned the local CBS affiliate.

The letter surprised me, primarily because I had not applied for the scholarship. I received the award because one of my professors nominated me. I have to admit that before that occurrence, I had never thought much about private philanthropy. I was almost mystified that someone I did not know (Mr. Fetzer) would give me money to pursue my studies, with nothing expected in return. Much to my delight, I also received the scholarship during my senior year.

The amount of money granted by the scholarship, while helpful, was not huge. I believe an even bigger benefit than the money itself was the confidence in my abilities the scholarship spurred.

Many of my local contemporaries likely think of the broadcasting industry or the Detroit Tigers baseball team that he once owned when they hear the name John E. Fetzer. Personally, I think of Mr. Fetzer as someone who believed in aspiring students like me who showed potential.

Years later, when I returned to WMU to work as a development officer, I enjoyed some success in asking alumni and friends to establish scholarship funds like the one created by Mr. Fetzer. In retrospect, it was not difficult to ask for the gifts. I had personally experienced the positive impacts of WMU scholarship funds created by private benefactors.

That's my story, the one that motivates me as a fundraiser. What's yours?

Presenting an Opportunity

I want to re-emphasize a point I first mentioned in Chapter Eight. Perhaps I am a tad naïve, but I am frequently surprised when I contact a potential new supporter and the prospect refuses to meet with me.

Typically, my reaction is:

"Why wouldn't someone want to meet with me? We have amazing students, great faculty, and exemplary programs. I can't imagine why anyone would not want to learn more and get involved."

Is this a Pollyanna approach? Perhaps, but I *really* believe it!

Now, I am realistic enough to know that not everyone I contact will share my enthusiasm. I do know, however, that people in general enjoy connecting with individuals who are passionate about *something*. Many times, that passion can be contagious. Sometimes people will meet with you simply because they are intrigued by your energy. They want to visit with you, in person, just to see for themselves if you are "for real."

Perhaps you share an approach similar to mine. If not, I hope you can find a way to tap into your own personal brand of enthusiasm.

As facilitators of philanthropic investments, we fundraisers are a remarkably fortunate lot. How many other professions can boast that they are *truly* engaged in helping people make the world a better place?

When I conduct qualification calls, my job is to introduce my prospect to some of the great life-changing and transformational work being done by my organization. Since our work—and I'm sure the work of your nonprofit—is pretty amazing, the task is actually fairly easy. After all, it's *not* about us.

In the end, development officers are merely connectors and conduits (albeit skillful ones). We are there to help the donor make a difference. What an amazing and beautiful privilege!

Our Journey Concludes, and Begins

I sincerely hope the observations, tools, and techniques I have shared with you in this book will be helpful to you. I believe, when employed with a disciplined and strategic focus, they will benefit you throughout your fundraising career.

In Chapter Eight, you may recall the "lungo viaggio," or long journey, reference I used to describe relationship building with prospective major donors. In a similar vein, I hope our journey together through this book has encouraged you—or perhaps even inspired you—to step up your major gift program with a healthy dose of donor qualification visits.

I know I am not the first development practitioner to make the statement, "If you don't know 'em, you can't ask 'em." Regardless of who said it first, the statement remains a very elemental but essential fundraising truth.

I wish you the very best in your resource development efforts and hope to hear about some of your triumphs in future days.

To Recap

◆ There are donors who will give and thank you for the opportunity.

◆ Look to colleagues and other resources for support.

◆ Be ready to share your personal story.

◆ The lungo viaggio ends, and begins.

Appendix A

College of Education
Office of Development
2308 Sangren Hall
Kalamazoo, MI 49008

www.wmich.edu/coe

Sherie Veramay
Director of Development
(269) 387-4593

Appendix B

College of Health and Human Services
www.website.edu
(987) 555-1234

Leadership

Dean	June Jones (june.jones@website.edu)
Associate Dean	Bill Smith (bill.smith@website.edu)

Statistics
Enrollment, Fall 2010

Undergraduate	2,129
Graduate	760
Total	2,889

Degrees Awarded, 2009-10

Bachelor's	322
Master's	282
Doctoral	17
Total	621

Total Alumni	***15,499***

Faculty/Staff, Fall 2009

Full-time faculty	89
Faculty chairs	6
Part-time faculty	60
Adjuncts/visiting professors	14
Graduate assistants	50
Regular staff	43

Grants, 2009-10

Number of grants received	17
Value of grants received	$3,436,375

College of Health and Human Services Fast Facts

◆ National Magazine ranks CHHS occupational therapy, physician assistant, and speech pathology graduate programs among the top fifty programs of their kind in the nation. Rehabilitation counseling, social work, and audiology are also ranked among the best graduate schools in the nation.

◆ Academic programs are housed in a high-tech building that facilitates progressive methods of teaching, learning, and research. It is the first building in (region) to meet Leadership in Energy and Environmental Design for Existing Buildings (LEED-EB) standards, and its (year) gold-level certification distinguishes it as the most highly rated higher-education building in the United States.

◆ Through CHHS affiliates—the Unified Clinics and the Center for Disability Services—students practice clinical skills, and a broad population of community members receive specialized health care. These enterprises serve 1,800 patients per week in over 80,000 appointments annually.

◆ The Department of Blindness and Low Vision Studies is the oldest and largest—and regarded as one of the best programs of its kind—in the world. Faculty members are engaged in groundbreaking national research on safety issues related to quiet cards and traffic roundabouts, which impact the safety of persons with blindness and low vision.

◆ The Department of Speech Pathology and Audiology (SPPA) was one of the nation's earliest clinics for the study and treatment of speech disorders and the preparation of speech therapists. Its founder, Dr. Charles Speaker, was a pioneer in the field, known worldwide for his innovative treatment for stuttering. The SPPA graduate program, currently ranked thirty-eighth in the nation, was the first in (state) and one of the first six in the nation to gain accreditation.

◆ Website U's Holistic Health Care Program is one of only four similar programs in the country and offers both an undergraduate minor and graduate certificate that foster "holism" within health care and across other disciplines.

◆ The college's occupational therapy department is the first and oldest non-teacher education program at Website U—its founding in 1922 initiated Website U's expansion from a teachers' college to a comprehensive institution of higher learning—and the highest-ranking occupational therapy program in (state) by *National Magazine*, 2008.

◆ The CHHS physician assistant program is the first to be established with legislative approval and funding appropriation in (state) and has one of the highest pass rates in the country for its national licensure exam.

◆ The School of Social Work's *Journal Publication* has served the profession for thirty-five years, reaching national and international audiences through subscriptions and digital database access.

◆ Established in (year), the Specialty Program in Alcohol and Drug Abuse was the first of its kind in (state) and the first university-based training clinic in (state) to address the criminal justice population of substance abusers.

Appendix C

July 27, 2012

Mr. James Jackson
240 Water Street
Anytown, USA

Dear James:

It was a pleasure meeting with you at Anytown City Hall. I really appreciate your great enthusiasm for and continuing interest in Western Michigan University. I enjoyed providing you with current information on programs of interest to you.

Congratulations on your career success, and thank you for your potential interest in visiting campus at a future convenient time. I think you would be a very interesting and well received speaker and have already suggested the possibility of a visit to our political science faculty.

Since you mentioned a question about the WMU-Cooley Law School affiliation, I did a bit of research that I think will answer your question (see enclosed article). As I understand it, there is currently a 15-credit limit for Cooley courses at the WMU downtown Grand Rapids campus, but hopefully that will soon change.

Again, James, thank you for your time and interest. I look forward to our future contact.

Sincerely,

John J. Greenhoe
Director of Development

Enc.

PLEASE CALL ME THE NEXT TIME YOU'RE IN MICHIGAN!
(555) 123-7890

Index

If you enjoyed this book, you'll want to pick up the other books in the CharityChannel Press **In the Trenches**™ series.

And dozens more coming soon!

www.CharityChannel.com

And now introducing **For the GENIUS® Press,** an imprint that produces books on just about any topic that people want to learn. You don't have to be a genius to read a **GENIUS** book, but you'll sure be smarter once you do!

Made in the USA
San Bernardino, CA
08 April 2016